CELEBRATING FAMILY HISTORY

An
Anthology of
Prize-winning Stories
Sponsored by the
Southern California
Genealogical Society

Edited
and
with an
Introduction by
Beth Maltbie Uyehara

HERITAGE BOOKS
2007

HERITAGE BOOKS

AN IMPRINT OF HERITAGE BOOKS, INC.

Books, CDs, and more—Worldwide

For our listing of thousands of titles see our website
at
www.HeritageBooks.com

Published 2007 by
HERITAGE BOOKS, INC.
Publishing Division
65 East Main Street
Westminster, Maryland 21157-5026

International Standard Book Number: 978-0-7884-4084-5

About SCGS

*The Southern California Genealogical Society
was founded in 1964 to serve the interests
of genealogists living in Southern California,
as well as those in other areas whose research
concerns Southern California. The Society is based
in Burbank, and has one of the largest private U.S.
genealogical libraries west of the Mississippi.
The library is open to the public at no charge.
In 2000, with the goal both of promoting
genealogical research and of encouraging
researchers everywhere to "put it in writing,"
SCGS launched a family-history writing contest,
open to all. Since then, we have received
many hundreds of entries from seven countries
and from all across the U.S. and Canada.
The quality of the writing has been so high,
and the stories have been so interesting,
that we decided the authors
deserved a wider audience.
This book is the result.
We hope it will inspire family historians
everywhere to start writing!*

So. Calif. Genealogical Society,
417 Irving Drive, Burbank, CA 91504-2408
(818) 843-7247
To learn more about the Society
or the writing contest,
visit the Website at www.scgsgenealogy.com

Contents

Acknowledgements

At the top of the list of people to thank are Thomas Curwen,
former deputy editor of the <u>Los Angeles Times Book Review</u>,
now editor of the <u>Outdoors</u> section of The Times;
and Megan Smolenyak Smolenyak,
the lead researcher of the PBS television series <u>Ancestors</u>,
the author of three popular books on genealogy,
and a contributing editor for <u>Heritage Quest Magazine</u>.
Mr. Curwen has been a judge every year since we began,
and he has offered us invaluable advice
and encouragement as we have developed and refined
the contest. Ms. Smolenyak has been a judge for four of our five
years and has been a friend of the project from the beginning.
Many thanks also go to our other judges: journalist, poet,
and educator Terri Niccum, and freelance writer
Jean Chapman Snow, who became a judge in 2004
after winning prizes in the first four contests.
Doug Miller, the former president of SCGS, supported our
efforts to get the contest off the ground in 2000,
and backed up his enthusiasm with hard work.
Mr. Miller was one of the many unsung SCGS volunteers
who have put in long hours managing the printings
and mailings of contest-related materials.
And SCGS board member Louise Calaway has been
the vital "enabler" of the contest since its inception.
Neither the contest nor the book would exist without her.
The proofreading team of Sharon Ford, Kay Irwin,
Dennis McCargar, Vieve Metcalfe, Jean Chapman Snow, and
SCGS President Pam Wiedenbeck put in hard work
and long hours poring over the manuscript.
My thanks also go to Kelley Williams—for her invaluable
editorial insights and advice, and her never-wavering
encouragement. And I can't tell you how much I appreciate
my husband, Paul, for putting up with this whole thing!

Acknowledgments

Introduction

Is there a difference between genealogy and family history? The terms are used interchangeably so often that the lines have become blurred—but I think there is a real distinction.

Genealogists are primarily engaged in investigating and verifying the milestone events of ancestors' lives: births, deaths, marriages, migrations. They are on a quest for information that has been lost to the family.

Family historians, on the other hand, want to understand and preserve the everyday details of personalities and family interactions. They may not know for sure when or where Grandma was born, but they know what she was like as a person: They remember her voice, what she liked for breakfast, and what made her laugh. If they are lucky, they'll also know a few details of her life's journey, but that's just icing on the cake. What really counts is understanding who the person was who made that journey: what it felt like to be Grandma. What the world looked like through her eyes.

If you think of family life as a coloring book, genealogists are the ones drawing the outlines, while family historians are the ones adding the colors and the shading that bring the picture to life.

In practical, day-to-day terms, then, family historians *record* and *preserve*—and, often, what they are recording and preserving is information they already possess—particularly, family lore and family artifacts. The lore can include their own or others' memories, anecdotes, oral histories, or legends passed down from generation to generation. Artifacts can include writings, such as diaries, letters, biographies, histories, and memoirs; school or military mementoes; news clippings; ephemera; photos; needlework; scrapbooks; etc.

Genealogy requires serious research skills. Researchers need to understand the nature of evidence, be able to evaluate their own and others' research, and learn how to present their own research in ways that can withstand scrutiny by other researchers. Tough stuff.

Some family historians have little interest in researching remote generations—just as some genealogists don't care much about preserving stories of more recent family life. Most of us straddle the divide, however, and obviously, the two are closely intertwined. Most of us want to recover and understand as much of the past as possible—but we also want to preserve records of our family's recent generations and experiences.

THERE ARE SOME MARVELOUS examples in this book of ways to combine the two mindsets—but this anthology is primarily about family history. It's by and for family historians and the general reader. Genealogical research is secondary to the attempt by these authors to capture the lives and characters of the people and places they are writing about.

Even when the stories in this anthology are based on sophisticated genealogical research, you'll see that the emphasis is on the lives and experiences of the people who were being researched, not on the research process.

One of the purposes of this anthology (and of the writing contest on which it is based) is to demonstrate the variety of ways in which family history can be recorded and preserved. Another purpose, equally important, is to try to inspire family historians to take the plunge themselves and start writing down the stories they already know.

Because, by far the most effective way to preserve the things you know about your family's history is through the written word.

There is a famous proverb: *When a person dies, a library dies with them.* We all wish we had "listened more to Grandma's stories," or thought to ask questions of our elders when we had the chance. We realize, when it is too late, how much family history we have lost with each passing.

What we often don't appreciate, however, is how much we still possess. We may have lost Grandma and Grandpa, but we haven't lost our memories of who they were, what they were like, and, usually, a few stories about their lives. This is the kind of information that no future genealogist, no matter how skilled, will ever be able to recapture through public records. The only way it will be preserved is if it's written down by the people who know it first-hand, from personal experience—that is, by you and me.

Fifty years from now, will your grandchildren or great-grandchildren be wishing they could listen to *your* stories about your parents and siblings and neighbors and hometown, and what it was like to grow up in (check one) the 1940s, '50s, '60s, '70s, '80s, etc.? The answer to this is, "Yes, they will." But they won't have to kick themselves for not listening harder, or not asking the right questions, if you write down your family stories now.

And, as this book demonstrates, you don't have to write thick volumes, and you don't have to write like you're in a high school English class trying for an "A," to preserve your family history. You just have to write. Use your own language and "voice": You're not trying to impress anyone—just to record as accurately and honestly as you can the information you have about your family.

You can write short accounts, such as you'll find in this book, or put together a notebook full of observations and reminiscences. Brief accounts—even a few paragraphs—can provide vital records of people whose lives and personalities would otherwise be forgotten. Go through your old photo albums and write little biographies of the people you remember. Write about your own life. It's a funny thing, but the more you write, the more you'll remember.

In other words—be the kind of ancestor you wish you had!

SINCE WE BEGAN our family-history writing contest five years ago, we have received a cumulative total of more than five hundred entries, with the number of entries growing each year. In

2004 alone, we had about one hundred-sixty entries. To compile this anthology, I went back and read every story submitted to the contest since 2000—and I realized just how tough a job our judges have had. Many of the stories in this book were prize winners, but I also included a lot that were not, because they were just too interesting to leave out. The vast majority of the stories in this book (over thirty of the forty-some) have never been published before.

I tried to include as great a variety of styles, "voices," and approaches as possible, to demonstrate that when it comes to family-history writing, the important "rule" is to *Just Do It*, as the ads say.

There were a number of recurring themes among the stories, which helped me organize the material, but there was only room to include a few of these themes. And, as you will discover as you read this collection, many stories touch on several themes, and could have fit in several sections.

But ultimately, every story in this book ended up there simply because I was moved by it in some way—it made me laugh out loud, or it made me think (always a challenge!), or it made me sad, or it made me mad. Sometimes, a story just lingered in my mind and would not go away. . . .

I thank all these writers for sharing their stories with us, and I hope you will be as moved by their accounts as I was. (And, I hope that some of you will be inspired to write *your* stories down and send them to us for our next contest. For more information on that, check out page *iii*.)

And now, I will get out of the way and let you get going. Because this book is really about the sheer pleasure of reading—so get comfy, relax, and enjoy these remarkable, often touching, sometimes amazing, real-life, family-history stories.

— *Beth Maltbie Uyehara*
August, 2005

Dedicated
to
Louise Calaway

". . . for all you do
for SCGS"

Character
Sketches

All history is subjective.
In other words, there is properly no history,
only biography.
— Ralph Waldo Emerson

GRANDMA IVANOFF

by Michele Ivy Davis
Palm Harbor, Florida
2004

M y Grandma Ivanoff could tell the future with a deck of playing cards. She would sit on the edge of her bed arranging the cards face down in a special pattern on the soft surface. Then she would turn them over slowly, one by one, studying the results, her face impassive. Sometimes, if we were gathered around, she would tell my mother what they meant, but it was a slow process because she had to look most of the words up in her dog-eared Russian/English dictionary.

She consulted the cards every day, in much the same way my mother consulted her horoscope in the newspaper. But my grandmother made it clear that it was not a game and she never read the cards just because we asked her to.

It made me uneasy when, as I sat on the floor watching her, she would abruptly uncurl her wire-rim glasses from behind her ears and gather up the partially turned cards.

"What do they say?" I would ask.

"Nothing. Go," she would answer, her mouth a grim line as she put them back in their box. Then she shooed me away with a wave of her hands.

She never told us what the cards foretold on those occasions, but it must have been terrible, and I would wait for one of us to be struck dead or the house to burn down.

My grandmother came to the United States in 1955 from Harbin, China, where she and my grandfather settled after the Russian Revolution. She arrived at our house in a quiet bustle, speaking words we didn't understand, her hair pulled tight in a bun and a musty suitcase spilling presents for us, the grandchildren she had never seen. My younger sisters and I happily tried on the identical turquoise brocade Chinese jackets and small "diamond" rings she brought. Although my jacket was given away long ago, I still have the ring in my jewelry box.

Grandma Ivanoff probably wouldn't receive a second glance on the street—a short, elderly woman, slightly bowlegged, with a fondness for shoes from discount stores, the silver and gold kind with multi-colored rhinestones glued to the tops; she wore them with ankle socks. She was rarely without an apron over her housedress or a tissue for eyes that seemed to water slightly but constantly. Her dentures clicked when she talked and her eyes crinkled in the corners when she smiled.

But when Agapia Ivanoff went to church, she transformed herself. She put on lipstick and stockings, tossed a little fur over her shoulders—one that still had the animals' heads on it—and got out her good purse. She swished when she walked, and smelled like roses.

Later, I came to wonder at her need to attend the far-away Russian Orthodox Church in downtown Washington, D.C., because it was such a difficult trip for her—two bus rides and a long walk each way, all in high heels. Her church offered only a few chairs, so she stood through the whole service because the seats were "for the old people." Going to church took four or more hours.

3

Maybe her connection to the church dated from my grandmother's early life when it helped her locate her husband after the Russian Revolution in 1919. As the wife of an officer in the Czar's army, she and the other wives were in danger. They were instructed to take one small bag and to appear to be going on an outing. She sewed money and jewelry into her clothes, took my infant father, and boarded the Trans-Siberian Railway with the other wives. They crossed frozen Russia, finally arriving in Harbin, China. Meanwhile, their soldier husbands crossed China and Mongolia, almost starving in the Gobi Desert. Without telephones or mail, my grandmother had no idea where my grandfather was, so she posted messages for him in churches along the way. He eventually found her through those messages.

Seeing her calmly sitting on the bus, no one would know that at the end of World War II, the Soviet Russians came looking for those who had fought against them. They took her husband from her house, and she never saw or heard from him again. Nor would they have known that she had a career as an operating room nurse long before women had careers; that she traveled thousands of miles to live in our household of strangers, not speaking a word of English. Nor that she stubbornly smoked her whole life, in a time when women just didn't do that. (She would pinch out an unfinished cigarette and put it back in the pack to smoke again later.)

One of the few times she let her natural reserve drop was on her sixty-fifth birthday. My sister and I decided to give her an American birthday cake with sixty-five candles on it. In our minds, it was to be a wonderful thing. In reality it was . . . well, something else.

We began lighting the candles and soon realized that they were burning much too quickly. We started to giggle. The heat from the melting candles spread wax over the top of the cake. We frantically struck matches as the wax covered the top of the cake and dripped down the sides. When my grandmother came into the kitchen to see what was happening, a smile slowly crept across her face. She started to snicker, then chuckle, and finally laughter bubbled over the hand she held in front of her mouth as she tried to hold it all in.

Tears rolled from her eyes while we peeled the wax from her piece of the wonderful cake. I don't think it was a birthday she ever forgot. I know I didn't.

My Grandma Ivanoff died many years ago, but the lessons I learned from her remain with me still: Sometimes life isn't fair, but you deal with it and go on; you are never too old to learn something new; and sometimes you have to pick wax out of your birthday cake.

COUSIN LEM

by Maude I. Parker
Brooklyn, New York
2004

Into the struggle for survival by our Caribbean immigrant families in Harlem, the New Deal injected hope. At the same time, an undercurrent of rage existed against the ineffectual League of Nations, which seemed to lack the will to protect Ethiopia from the Fascist expansion of Italy. Friends and some Roman Catholic family members left the church because of what they perceived to be church support of Italy's genocide of Ethiopians. Daily street-corner and step-ladder oratory railing against European imperialism and degradation of Africans in the diaspora was the backdrop of my life. In this vortex of socio-political ferment, my cousin Lem loomed large.

He and my father had a ritual greeting dance. On seeing my father, Lem would exclaim, "*Ecce homo!* Behold the man!" Then Daddy would grab some chalk and mark a spot in front of Lem and say, "Mark a chalkline; mark a chalkline." It was said that West Africans honored guests by chalking the ground in front of them.

When they would drink, they always poured a drop of the alcoholic beverage on the floor for the spirits of our ancestors before they took a drink. My older sister, Elaine, and I loved this theater.

Lem was born in Antigua, British West Indies, in the last decade of the 19th Century. His mother was my mother's aunt and his father was my father's cousin. He was educated in schools as far as a descendant of slaves was allowed to go. He sought his fortune in the expanding 20th Century economy of Santo Domingo before emigrating to the United States. Because of his race, he encountered barriers in both places to employment where he could utilize his mathematical and accounting skills. Discrimination was a heavy yoke for him.

Judging by my father, he was a little under six feet tall, erect. His was a chocolate-syrup complexion, chiseled features, and eyes that seemed to smile . . . movie-star handsome. Speaking a Churchillian type of English with a Caribbean lilt, he was referred to as an "English Dict" (because of his diction). He was also fluent in Spanish. He was well read and opinionated. Men sought his company and his ideas on everything. Lem was an effective debater. Women gravitated to him whenever he entered a room. His suave manners and his knowledge of literature enthralled them.

He was a stylish *bon vivant* of that day. His hair was close-cropped, neat. Always *au courant* in dress, with suede or leather gloves, white silk scarf, and a derby in cooler weather. In warmer times, Lem used a variety of straw and Panama hats to accessorize the white flannels and sharkskin Gatsbyesque attire of the men in the Harlem Glitterati.

Children adored him. He did not hold to the prevailing dictum of the day that children should be seen and not heard. Whereas most adults gave children pennies or nickels, Lem gave us quarters. When Elaine and I were in his presence, he focused on us. He requested that we play our most recently learned piano pieces on the upright Walter player piano in our living room. He listened to our recitations of poems we learned at school. He seemed to think we were special because his two cousins, Leonard and Octavia, our parents, had produced us. He reminded us that Daddy's sister, Muriel, was a well-known supervising teacher in St. Kitts/Nevis, and that we could not achieve less than she. He said American education could make us women of influence. His stories and jokes were geared to our level of understanding. We loved him.

Mama fawned over him and delighted in preparing his favorite Antiguan foods. She never failed to counsel him that his playboy lifestyle and liquor were damaging his health. At times, she expressed shame with his reputation as a thief, his having been discharged from his position as head of the Usher Board in Rush Memorial Church for pilfering their funds for his high living.

By the mid-1930s, he was drinking heavily, but since he inherited the look of agelessness from his maternal side, the ravages of abuse were not apparent.

Few people understood the dynamic of alcoholism as a disease at that time; there was no help for Cousin Lem, who was caught in a destructive downward spiral. Mama told him not to visit any more unless he were sober. One Sunday, he came roaring to our apartment on 140th Street, noisily banging on the door. Mama told him to go away, but he did not accept refusal/rejection. While Mama, Elaine, and I cowered inside in silence, he proceeded to tear the door off the hinges, shouting that he could not be kept out of his family's house. Then, exhausted and spent, he did not enter, but turned and left.

Daddy was speechless and very concerned that our beloved cousin had terrified his family and damaged his home. "Liquor made Lem do it. Liquor is the ruination of you men," Mama lamented. After my father found him and chastised him, Cousin Lem was tearfully contrite, and begged my mother to forgive him. After that, he was not allowed to visit unless Daddy was present. We saw less of him, but our love for him remained constant.

Eventually, he married an American-born, Josephine Baker look-alike who was the object of widespread jealousy. It was rumored that Lem continued to visit other women.

Then he became ill with intestinal problems. Some Antiguan

expatriates claimed that he was "fixed" (poisoned). He lingered for months. We visited regularly, sad that he was suffering. It could have been the effects of chronic alcoholism, but the word was abroad that his death was suspicious. He died as World War II was beginning.

At the cemetery, as his casket was being lowered into the grave, one of the ropes broke, causing the casket to tilt precariously to the right, the lower part angling downward. Audible gasps escaped from everyone. Cousin Bernice, our primary wailing mourner, jumped in a fit of animated passion, almost sliding down into the open grave. As she was grabbed by some men, she screamed, "Oh, Lem, you lived crooked, you died crooked, and now you are going down in your grave crooked!" Her comico-dramatic behavior provoked smothered laughter, along with tears.

That night, I dreamed that Cousin Lem kept repeating the number 309 to me. I told Mama about the dream, and she bet that number with the local runner in the morning. She won a substantial sum of money: 309 has been my lucky number ever since.

GOING TO THE DANCE

by Gina Lee
Burbank, California
2004

Grandmother was born on the island of Cozumel in 1890. I find this very obliging of her, because I can remember her age by simply taking the last two digits of whatever year it is, and adding ten.

Every birthday she seems to shrink a little bit. Her long, horsey face now looks more apple-ish. But in a roomful of wheelchair grandmas, she's easy to pick out. She's the cute one with the jaunty bow on her silky white hair. She's the one conducting an invisible orchestra.

We look alike, Grandma and I. Same eyes, same nose, same mouth, same expression. My genes seem to have skipped my parents entirely and bounced back a generation. I have my youth, of course, but I have never had as much spirit.

I call her Anita now; it's easier. How could she remember me? She doesn't even remember my father. She had seven children in all; five are still living. She only remembers her oldest son, who lives in the home with her. He is only in his seventies. A stroke robbed him of his mind. Mostly he sits and cries, but his mother still takes care of him. She orders the nurses around like a general, seeing that her little boy is taken care of.

"Happy Birthday, Anita," I tell her, handing her the slippers and duster Mama wrapped. Mama bought them, too—I never know what to get someone who lives in a wheelchair. "You're one-hundred-three now. How do you feel?"

But she is already busy unwrapping the packages, broken fingernails trying to break the Scotch tape.

"No! This is my present," she snaps when I try to help, and then smiles to show there's no hard feelings. "I have to be careful with the wrapping. Dad doesn't like it when you just rip it open. If you press it, you can use it over again."

She gets the duster open, unfolds it, and fingers it reverently.

"Oh, it's lovely!" she coos. "Dad always buys me the prettiest things."

"Last month when I was here, we had a long discussion about music," Mama tells me, while Grandma opens her other present. Mama always brings a tape recorder and plays music while she visits her mother-in-law. Her needle flies over a bit of cross-stitch as she talks. "She was very coherent, last time."

The slippers are open and Grandma is staring at them blankly.

"They're slippers!" Mama announces gaily. She drops her sewing and slips them over her hands. They dance across the table, and Grandma glares at her.

"They go on your <u>feet</u>," she says severely, as you would speak to a toddler. Mama takes off the slippers and hands them over.

"I went to Mexico," I say brightly, trying to fill up the silence. "I went on a cruise. Do you remember Mexico?"

I'm not sure if she hears me or not. Her eyes are good, but her hearing is mostly gone. I switch ears, just in case.

"Are you going to the dance?" she asks, squeezing my hand. When I am with her, I am always touching her, her face, her hair, her arms, trying to trigger some spark of recognition. She acts like we're good friends, at any rate. Now we are holding hands.

"What dance, Grandma?" I slip and call her Grandma, but she takes no notice. She knows she's Anita, no matter what I call her.

"I was just thinking about him," she says wistfully. "I wonder if he's thinking about me, too."

"I'm sure he is," I agree. If she won't come into the present with me, I'll slip into the past with her.

"I think he's probably suffering just as much as me," she goes on. "He might act tough, but I know he hurts, too."

How far back are we going this time? I search my mind desperately for a place, a time, a person.

Mama tries to help. "You know she's not talking about her husband," she says. "She never loved him like that."

No, not Grandfather, the American doctor she married in Guanajuoto. Not the man who took her as a spoiled only child from a wealthy family and plunged her into poverty across the Texas border. Not the man she bullied for more than fifty years.

A tear fills her eye, threatening to spill over.

"Don't cry, Anita," I tell her.

She wipes the tear away and smiles. "I think he must cry, too," she says. "Not in front of anybody, of course. But I think he probably sheds a tear or two, when he's alone."

Suddenly it hits me. The gambler. She's talking about the gambler. I don't remember his name. I don't remember if she ever told me his name. I only heard bits and pieces of the story. He was someone she met before Grandfather, someone older and dashing and handsome who drank too much. Her father refused to let her marry him. She was too young and he was a wastrel. When was it—1907, 1908? There was some sort of incident, never clearly defined, and her father had pulled a gun on him.

"Are you going to the dance?" she asks me now.

"There isn't any dance, " I explain patiently. "That was a long time ago."

Mama gets out her recent batch of photos. Her purse bulges with her cameras. She carries three. She says she needs different ones for different shots. I don't know. It's all very technical and mysterious, lighting and lenses and things. She starts showing the pictures to Grandma, who comments politely on each one.

I'm still thinking about her father and the gun. It was her stepfather she was so devoted to. She always said he was her real father, there wasn't any "step" about it. Her biological father had disappeared in the jungle in Cozumel when she was a baby. He was a New Yorker by way of Germany, Baron von Stein, and her widowed mother had married an American who was out there looking for something, oil, I think.

Grandma knew about guns. When my uncle showed us his gun collection, she grabbed a little snub-nosed pistol.

"That's a derringer. I used to have one of those," she said.

"It looks like a toy," I remarked.

"Not at all. It's a lady's pistol. It only has one bullet. You carry it in your purse."

"You carried a gun?"

"Of course. A lady has to carry a pistol to defend her honor. You don't have to aim it or anything. When a nasty character grabs you, you just smile and slip it out of your purse. While he's busy love-making, you just push it against his chest and give it a little squeeze."

My uncle took back the gun in a hurry and checked the chamber. He relaxed visibly after he assured himself it wasn't loaded. Grandmother was ninety-five at the time, and there was always the possibility that she might suddenly go senile while she was armed.

Mama is putting away her pictures and Grandma is talking to me again.

"I love you," she says. She gestures toward Mama. "I like her a lot. She's OK, with her pictures and her sewing. But I <u>love</u> you." She squeezes me again.

Who am I supposed to be now? Maybe she has gone back before the gambler. It's a happier place, at least. I ransack my memories for clues. She had a pony and a dog and lots of dolls. I remember her talking fondly about her bulldog, and I always pictured a wheezing, bow-legged, sweet old thing. Then I saw a picture of her and her dog. It was a pit bull.

But that was too far back. She hadn't had any friends when she was little. Boarding school. She had gone to a Catholic boarding school. I remember she told me about sneaking smokes in the bathroom. Somewhere in her teens there was music, too. She had studied opera and was pretty good at it, but when she was invited to join an opera company, her father wouldn't let her. No daughter of his would shame him by going into The Theater.

There had been tears and pleading, but her dad was firm. He had allowed her to study music because it was a nice accomplishment for a young lady to have. She wasn't supposed to do anything so base as to sing for money. I never heard whether he pulled a gun on the opera director or not.

I do know that Grandma eventually had to take money for her music. During the Depression, when her doctor husband was being paid in chickens and garden truck—when he was paid at all—she opened up a music school. She had her own orchestra and she taught me piano and voice when I was little. That orchestra in the border town must have been a good memory for her, because she still directed it from the day room in the home.

"Are you going to the dance?" she asks me again, and now I know that I'm going. I'm going to be just like this grand lady I'm sitting with. I'm going to dance my way through forever. Whatever obstacles life throws at me, I'm going to bang away at until my path is clear.

"Of course I'm going to the dance, Anita," I tell her. "I wouldn't miss it for anything. You know how I love to dance."

I've made Grandma happy. Her smile lights up her face like Christmas. I would tell a million lies to see that smile again.

"Well, good!" she exclaims. "I knew you'd go. I knew you wouldn't miss a dance."

It's time to go. Mama is laughing at us with her eyes—three generations of women, all dancing our way through time.

Local
Color

There is nothing like returning
to a place that remains unchanged
to find the ways in which you yourself have altered.
— Nelson Mandela,
"A Long Walk to Freedom"

Clydeside Living, 1944-1949

by George Smith
Dunbartonshire, Scotland
2004

In the evenings of the 13th and 14th of March 1941, the Luftwaffe raided my hometown of Clydebank; this was an industrial town of 50,000. Home to the Singer sewing machine factory, and John Brown's shipyard, where the *Queen Mary* and *Queen Elizabeth* were built. The records show that after two nights of bombing only eight houses were undamaged. Our house received a direct hit, everything was gone, all we had was the clothes we were wearing. Initially we were given clothes provided by the American Red Cross. If you saw someone dressed like a Yank you knew he, or she, had been "Bombed out," as we said. Since then we had been living with a family friend in Dumbarton.

I have my late father's Identity Card from World War II, and his change of residence from 47 Townend Road, Dumbarton to 21 Peters Square, Clydebank, is dated the 6th of September 1944. That must have been approximately the day we moved into our prefab, and I would have been eight years old. We stayed there until November 1949, five happy, happy years. It was a great place to grow up in. Always something going on, always something for wee boys to investigate.

Our prefab was only built to last ten years, just a temporary expedient, or so they said. However it would not be till 1967 that the last one was declared uninhabitable and eventually pulled down.

The houses were semi-detached, single-story buildings, arranged around a square, although it was actually oval in shape. The centre space in the square was just left empty, as the war was still being fought and there were more important things to do than landscape an area such as this. It was a natural playground, it didn't "belong" to anyone, you could dig holes, make huts, light fires, a real adventure playground.

Paths radiated out from the peripheral road, each path normally leading to two buildings on the right and two on the left, i.e. eight homes were serviced by each path.

Houses built in this style would nowadays be described as semi-detached bungalows; to us they were just "The Prefabs," never "the prefabricated houses." A concrete base was poured and a series of concrete combination vertical support and angled roof supports were dug in every eight feet or so round the base. These vertical supports had a groove in them into which concrete slabs were fitted, thus forming the walls, and, as far as I remember, there was no cavity wall present. The roof consisted of corrugated asbestos sheeting.

When you went in the front door there was a short entrance hall, or lobby. At the end of this there was, wonder of wonders, a bathroom complete with a toilet, wash hand basin and a bath, both of which had hot running water. My parents set up their first home in 1936, and this was the first bathroom they had ever had, and the first toilet that the family had never had to share.

To the right there were two bedrooms; you could get a double bed in each but not much else. Each of the bedrooms had a one-bar electric fire fitted to the wall as standard. On the left there was the

17

living room, with a coal fire. Off the living room there was a kitchen with a cooker (stove) and a sink which had hot and cold water; this hot running water in the kitchen and bathroom was nothing short of heaven. People forget how many Scots didn't have this facility sixty years ago. My parents were over the moon.

Initially, we were all very happy. However my parents, along with other tenants, noticed that the concrete floors were becoming damp; some houses were a lot worse than others. Eventually, after a lot of protesting, the council came up with a solution: All the floors would be coated with bitumen about two inches thick. Dead easy, you were told which day your house would be done, all the contents would have to be out by eight a.m., the cooker was disconnected and removed, all the doors were taken off. I can't remember about the bath or the toilet bowl—I assume they came out as well. However, if your day came and it was raining, the work was postponed until the next dry day, thus knocking everyone else back one more day.

The tar boiler was fired up, and once it was pourable, a gang of men with buckets of bitumen coated the floors. All you had to do was sit there with all your furniture around you until the foreman said the bitumen was set. Once they got the all-clear, the joiners came, cut the doors to size and refitted them. The cooker and bathroom fittings were also reinstated. You could then get your furniture back into the house. The council were not involved in either getting your furniture out or back in, that was your responsibility. A paradise for nosy neighbours, who had all day to see who had what.

That cured the damp floors, but the roof also required a "make over" as they say on the TV. Internally, when you looked up, it was similar to being inside a medieval cathedral, but only similar. Instead of oak beams we had concrete, and instead of a wooden roof we had asbestos sheet. However the aesthetics of the roof were not the main complaint. In the winter when it was very cold the heat used to rise and any moisture in the air would condense on the inside of the roof.

Either the moisture fell from the roof directly onto whoever was sitting under it, or it ran down the inside of the sloping roof and down the walls. Not only that, but the asbestos roof acted as a giant radiator, dissipating the heat from our coal fire to the heavens. More complaints to the town council.

Once more, it was a case of emptying everything out—well, not quite, the bath, toilet, sinks, and cooker were all allowed to stay. Once again by eight a.m. all the furniture had to be removed to allow the joiners in. This time they built a false ceiling of chipboard throughout the house, then you were allowed back in.

These two "modifications" took place in the summer months, but I distinctly remember the next one taking place in the middle of winter. The tiny one-bar electric fires in the bedrooms were only a token gesture, hence more complaints. An eight a.m. start again, both bedrooms to be cleared of furniture. This time the bricklayers knocked out most of the gable end of the house and re-built it with a fireplace in each room. There was hoar frost in the air and there we were with the gable end open to the elements.

There was always something happening: The workmen's huts in the centre of the square seemed to be permanent fixtures.

My father had never had a garden and neither had most of the neighbours, but I remember the pamphlets which had a drawing of a man driving a spade into the ground on it, and the motto "Dig for Victory." He followed the instructions and soon we had a really good vegetable garden, and a drying green, which was his pride and joy, it was like a bowling green.

After a couple of years we noticed that the water coming out the taps was discoloured, rusty. Initially, if you ran the tap it ran clear, which was OK for the cold, but not so good for the hot. The problem got worse and worse. Because of the war, copper was in very short supply, so the hot water storage tank had been made of galvanized iron, and the internal plumbing was also galvanized. Eventually we were told the house would have to be re-plumbed. You were told which day and the plumbers came in and re-plumbed the house, this time in copper. The furniture didn't have to be removed, just re-organized to give them access at eight a.m.

It made an improvement, but the rusty water still persisted. The main water supply pipes for the houses would have to be replaced. Along came a gang of workmen and they dug trenches from every house, following the run of the pipes, until all the pipes were exposed. It was like the Somme in the First World War, trenches linking all the houses. They seemed to lie open for weeks, I don't think Health and Safety regulations had been invented then. I don't remember the trenches being covered or warning notices being posted. We had a great time playing in those trenches. Eventually all the pipes were renewed and the trenches filled in.

But when my father came home from work the day the trench was dug across our drying green and saw the state his drying green was in, he nearly cried. "All that work for damn all," was the least of what he said.

There were swings in Whitecrook Park, which was great when it was dry, but not much use when it was raining. My young sister loved the swings, and pestered my mother, even when it was raining, to go to the swing park. As an electrician, my father was pretty good with his hands, so he decided to make a swing for my sister, but it had to be usable indoors. There was no actual door between the living room and the kitchen, just a doorway, so that was where the swing would be situated. He drilled into the concrete lintel and fitted to two large Rawlbolts with rings on the end. All my mother had to do was hook the swing onto the rings and my sister had her swing to play on. However he was not too confident that the concrete would take my weight so I was barred from the swing.

Eventually, my sister was now no longer a baby and we really needed another bedroom. Clydebank town council had built a lot of new houses between 1944 and 1949, so my parents managed to get a three bedroomed house in North Elgin street and that is where we moved. I missed the prefabs, even although they were despised in a way. "Oh, they stay in the prefabs," was a kind of put down. You were looked on as a sort of second-class citizen, why I'll never know. It wasn't our fault that Nazi Germany had blown our house from the face of the earth.

The allocation of the houses was through a system of points.

The larger the numbers of points you had, then the further up the housing list you were placed. When houses were available those at the top of the list got the houses, simple? Whether it was fair was another matter; you got points based on the number in your family, the circumstances under which you were living, what the husband's occupation was and how far he was living from his work. Those engaged on "Work of National Importance," got extra points. There were possibly other factors taken into consideration, but all I knew was that at that stage in the war, money in the bank did not normally make it any easier to get a house. This meant that the families were a right cross-section of the community. Labourers, tradesmen, dockers, works' managers, a chief naval architect from a shipyard, they were all living in the same area, and they just had to get on together.

Looking back on the prefabs, you could say it was a sort of social experiment, albeit unintentional. They had put people of different social and economic backgrounds into an environment where they all had to get on together, and I think we did so very well. Patches on clothes were the norm, clothing was rationed, food was rationed, hence no one was obese, everybody was in the same boat.

The Mud Sculpture— an Iowa Original

by Margaret Cullison
Grants Pass, Oregon
2004

O n the wall beside my computer hangs a photograph of a sculpture that inspires my creative efforts. In the picture, a woman lies with a baby nestled in her left arm, and the baby's arm reaches across her breast. Her right arm is outstretched, and the graceful folds of her garment flow over her body in the classical design of a Grecian statue. Mother and child are finely sculpted in every detail.

The full-size figures depict castaways from a shipwreck, and the sculpture is titled "Cast Up by the Waves." A 19th-Century novel of the same name, written by Sir Samuel White Baker, inspired the artist's creation.[1] What makes this work of art unique is that the woman and baby are made of mud and lie on the earth from which they were created. Within weeks, rain would wash the sculpture entirely away.

The time was April 1929, when the Great Depression had

already begun to impact farmers and farm communities in the Midwest. Over-production of crops continued following World War I, even though the need for farm goods had dwindled. Crop prices fell, annual income declined, and farmers found themselves in financial peril.[2]

News about an eccentric artist's arrival in town must have been a welcome diversion from their troubles. The newspaper in Harlan, a rural community of 4,000 thousand people in southwestern Iowa, featured two articles about the sculptor.

Other news on the day the second article appeared included mention of a farmer who found a wolf's lair while plowing his field, when he saw two wild eyes peering out at him. A local doctor made a house call to care for a worried couple's infant son. An advertisement pictured men's spring and summer underwear selling from $1 to $2.50. Another ad offered a used 1928 Chevrolet Cabroilet, "just as clean as a pin inside and out."[3]

The first article about the sculptor appeared on the front page and profiled J. B. McCord, who had arrived in town by train and pitched his tent by the railroad tracks. He set to work on his sculpture, ignoring curious onlookers, and explaining that he wanted to work alone and free of questions. He kept to himself until the sculpture was finished and then he was willing to talk. McCord said that he'd been educated at the Philadelphia School of Fine Arts, but the pressure of working in the critical art world had enervated him and caused health problems. He gave up that stressful life to become an itinerant creator of sculptures in mud.[4]

The artist worked near the water tower that supplied water for the trains passing through town, using the water that dripped from the tower to make the mud for his sculptures. A butcher knife was his only tool. Prairie grasses and scrub brush provided a backdrop for his art, and cattails grew in the swampy area below the tracks, closer to the Nishnabotna River. He made two sculptures, one of the woman and child and another of a soldier. Two photographs of the woman and child have been preserved.[5]

The owner of the property where the sculptures lay had tried to persuade McCord to mould his masterpieces in one of the display windows of his store. But the artist explained that he would be too much in the public eye there, and the distractions would bother him, preventing him from doing his best work.[6]

The only effort McCord made to preserve his sculptures was to pour oil over them after he'd finished them. Many townspeople came to see his creations in the short time they existed. Within a week, steady spring rains began washing away the figures, and they broke apart and dissolved back into the ground. People had trouble understanding this man who rejected public acclaim and didn't care about preserving his work. He seemed not to want fame or fortune, those two illusive desires that motivate many artists.

McCord left Harlan as quietly as he'd arrived, hopping a train to some other town, perhaps with a new subject for his ephemeral art already taking shape in his mind. He didn't care what people thought of him and understood that praise of his art had only temporary value. The fact that he completed the work to his own satisfaction must have been enough, art's true worth to him.

His feelings and motivations, the details of his story aren't known, as is the case with most people whose lives are over. But despite his desire for anonymity, J. B. McCord's artistic talent has been preserved in those few photographs. His will to create art for its own sake was recorded in the town's memory and its newspaper articles, giving his life a thin thread of immortality.

Resources

1. *The Harlan Tribune*, 17 April 1929, page 1.
2. *American Agriculture: Its Changing Significance, Farm Policy of the 20th Century*, U.S. Department of State, *http://countrystudies.us/united-states/economy-8.htm*.
3. *The Harlan Tribune*, 24 April 1929, page 3.
4. *The Harlan Tribune*, 17 April 1929, page 1.
5. Harlan Community Library archives and author's photograph
6. *The Harlan Tribune*, 24 April 1929, page 3.

Kriva Olka: A Mystery

By Melody Amsel-Arieli
Maalah Adumim, Israel
2003

Over one hundred years ago, my family lived in Olka, a tiny village that lies on the banks of the Laborce River in northeastern Slovakia. Few of their neighbors were Jewish. Like everyone there, they probably raised wheat and vegetables, tended chickens and geese, and kept a cow or two. Far-flung places like Olka were usually served by a single grocery store—and it was usually the Jews who ran it, selling candles, salt, flour, cones of sugar, sweets, oil, and soap. It was usually the Jews, too, who distilled plum liquor in their backyards, and then sold it out of their front room, their saloon. Running a saloon was a lucrative business, considering the local penchant for drinking.

Olkan Jews may have lived and worked alongside their Christian neighbors, but they preferred to study, pray, and celebrate in the company of their fellow brethren. What a sight they must have been on Shabbats and holidays when, weather permitting, they followed the winding road to Stropkov, caftaned and resplendent in their festive beaver *schtrelmels* (hats).

"Mother" Stropkov, about nine miles away, boasted the largest, most established Jewish community in northeastern Slovakia. She offered her "daughter" villages not only a synagogue, but also study groups, kosher food, a ritual bath, and the pleasures of communal prayer and celebrations. She also offered the services of her burial society and a consecrated cemetery.

Tragedy stuck Olka in the fall of 1893: Eight Jewish toddlers, all under the age of five, succumbed to grave illness. Zlata Siegelman died of bronchitis; three of the Moskivits children died of scarletina; Chajim Jozsef Grossberger, Gitte Berger, and Tezi and Sruel Amsel all died of pneumonia.

For some reason, these deaths were not reported when the children actually died. They appear in the Stropkov records[1] the following spring. Moreover, none of these children were buried in the Stropkov cemetery, as expected. They were buried in a place called Kriva Olka.

Once in Slovakia, I found Olka easily, and within a mile or so, I spotted a worn sign pointing down a narrow road: Kriva Olka.

A hundred years ago, Kirva Olka may have been a village. But today, it is barely a hamlet, only seven or eight wooden farmhouses obscured by towering trees and thick undergrowth. Curtains fluttered as we drove by. People had seen us arrive. Encouraged, we stopped, and our Slovak translator called out a greeting. An elderly woman approached warily, soon followed slowly by another and yet another. The three stared stony-eyed at us from behind the safety of their padlocked gate.

Yes, they remember the old Jewish cemetery—or maybe they remembered hearing about it. "Up over there, back behind the fields," they explained as they gripped the gate, "the Jews used to bury their children up there . . . there's nothing to see anymore, nothing left, not even the gravestones." They pointed toward the distant wooded hills behind them, then fell silent.

They averted their eyes; it was clear that they were waiting for us to leave their property.

But why were the children buried here in the hills of Kirva Olka instead of in consecrated ground? "The Jews were so poor," the oldtimers sighed, "that they could not afford to bury their children in Stropkov."

I wondered if this had been the real reason. Maybe other children in these families were also deathly ill and in need of care. Maybe the cold winter rains had already given way to snow and closed the roads until spring. Maybe the families simply did not have the strength to pull the wooden death carts by foot to Stropkov, though their burdens were so light.

We will never know. There are simply no Jews left to ask.

Resources

1. Latter-day Saints Library, Matrika, 1851-1901, Zidovska obec.

Sistersville Saturday Night

by Bonnie Copeland
Costa Mesa, California
2004

There is no mist on the river this evening. The air is cold and clear; the water is still as glass. I can see two Big Dippers, one in the sky and one in the river below. Waves sigh like sleeping babies as they break on the shore beneath my kitchen window.

Far off, silhouetted against the reflection of the moon on the water, the Sistersville Ferry glides between Ohio and West Virginia. In the one-hundred-sixty years since 1817, a Harmon has ferried wagons and cows and pigs and cars and foot passengers from one side of the river to the other, moving back and forth, six a.m. to six p.m., four trips an hour, seven days a week, April 1st through Christmas Eve. In the old days, Dib Harmon told me, the river was shallow enough for his great-grandpa to pole all the way across. Today, he only uses the pole to maneuver near the ferry landing; it takes a diesel engine to get through the current and past the shipping lanes dredged into the middle of the river. Things change very slowly here in the Ohio River Valley, but they still change.

I can barely see the ramshackle building across the river, but I know it houses the tackle and bait shop, post office, and cafe that constitute the city center of Fly, Ohio. The building is only a purple shadow, but the red neon sign on top illuminates the night sky like Las Vegas lights up the desert. The river is too wide for me to read the sign, but I can translate it from the backward cipher reflected by the water. "Fly Café—The Best Pie and We Don't Lie," shimmers in the black river and shatters into a million rubies as the ferry cuts through it.

Even though it's dark, it's only five p.m. The Fly Café is open until six on Saturday and the ferry runs until six, but the A&P market in Sistersville closed an hour ago. We haven't had dinner yet, and there's nothing in the refrigerator. The frost crunches under my bare feet as I step out onto the wooden porch. I cup my hands and call into the darkness, "Shannon! It's mother. Come home. We're going to Fly for take-out!"

A grimy seven-year-old appears out of the darkness. "Get your hat," I say, "and put on your galoshes. And for heaven's sake, wash your face. You look like you've been playing in the chicken yard again."

Shannon titters and hides a guilty smile behind a grimy hand. She goes inside to wash up at the kitchen sink. I follow her into the kitchen where I've left my parka draped over a chair. I put on my parka and rubber boots and grab my mittens and purse. I scrape the hoarfrost off of the windshield of our red Volkswagen and we head north on Rural Route 2 toward the Mason Dixon line and the ferry landing.

The ferry is waiting for us when we get to Wells Landing. I park our car under the shadow of the old oil well in Wells Landing Park and we wade through the mud to the ferry. I pay for our passage with two dimes that Dib slips into the silver coin changer at his waist.

"Hah," says Dib for the umpteenth time. "It's the pretty sistahs from Sistahsville, Wes' Virginia."

"She's my mother," Shannon says in disgust.

29

Dib's eyes twinkle and his teeth flash in the dark. "Oh. Looks young enough to be yo' sistah. And you look old enough to have a sistah her age, young lady. You do."

Shannon's frown turns into a smile. She can't wait to grow up.

Even though we're the only people on the ferry, Dib announces, "Passengers take theah seats. Ship ahoy!"

Shannon and I take a seat on the damp bench facing West Virginia. I put my arm around her to keep her warm. Dib lifts his pole from its hooks on the railing and carefully plants it in the water. The ferry pivots around the pole until we are facing our destination, Ohio.

Dib climbs into the pilot house, pokes his arm out of the window, and tugs on a rope. A single ear-splitting *broouch* explodes from the whistle. The diesel engine shudders and the ferry leaps forward. The smell of diesel fuel mixes with the cold air. I hold on to Shannon with one hand and the railing with the other so we aren't jerked into the water.

Ten feet out, the river closes in on us. Chill air wraps us like an ice cream cloak. I feel as if I cannot move. One arm is holding Shannon and the other is pinned to the rail. Even the *putt-putt* of the diesel is muffled by the heavy dampness. Wind reaches under my hat and caresses my hair. My cheeks are numb with cold; my eyelids burn. Tears freeze to my lashes and form a crystalline curtain between me and the rest of the world. The Sistersville Ferry slips into the moonlight as if it were moving into a dream.

Sometimes, in the morning I ride the ferry to work instead of driving twelve miles upriver to the New Martinsville Bridge. My eyes water in the cold. On winter mornings, the mountains on both sides of the river are shrouded by fog; the spindly tree skeletons that cover them float in my tears like ghostly apparitions. I exhale white puffs that disappear into the heavy mist, like the roads and buildings on the river banks. The fog is so thick I cannot see my hands. I am surrounded by the faint odor of fish and wet leaves. It is as if time has stopped, and I can imagine that the river looks the same as it did a hundred years ago.

With a bump and a thud the ferry scrapes against the mud flat of Fly landing. Shannon and I get off and slog across the frozen tire ridges toward the Café. Our path is lit by Fly's single street lamp and the red blush from the sign on the roof. A piece of plywood nailed on to a wooden lamp post by the side of the road announces, "Fly Café—The Best Pie and We Don't Lie," but the light over it has been burned out for years.

Dib shouts, "Gitcher food to go. This'll be mah last trip tonight ... I'll wait fuh you."

Shannon sits and waits in the grey skeleton of a wooden rocker. She knows that it'll take me a few minutes to open the front door.

I struggle with the warped door. It pops open. The warm air and light that pour out almost knock us over. I smell the blend of damp old building, burning wood from the pot-bellied stove, trucker sweat, the river, and food ... glorious food!

We pass the tables with their red-and-white checkered oilcloth covers and seat ourselves on chrome stools in front of the yellow Formica counter. Ella, the owner and waitress, slides a pencil from under her pink hairnet and asks, "Whad' ya gonna have?"

I ignore the stained menus in the metal holders at the rear of the counter. Instead, I check the chalkboard on the wall. Some of the specials are gone, erased from the board, but I can still read them. Earlier, we could have had pot roast and gravy or home-made meat loaf or fresh river fish, fried Cajun-style. I would have liked to have the fish, but people in Appalachia learn to live with disappointment. What's gone is gone.

"I'll have the roast turkey with mashed potatoes, gravy, and the fresh baked beets, to go, please," I say, "and could you put the rolls in a separate bag so we can eat them on the ferry?"

"You'll need extra rolls if'n you took the ferry," Ella says. She wipes her hands on the sides of her pink uniform and turns to Shannon. "Whad'll it be fuh you, li'l honey?"

Shannon doesn't have to look at the menu to know what she wants. She only eats one main dish. "Macaroni and cheese," she says, "to go."

Ella carves the turkey and covers the bottom of a metal pie plate with it. She plops two scoops of mashed potatoes on top of the turkey, dumps a scoop of corn bread dressing onto the potatoes, adds a spatula full of butter, pours gravy over everything and sets the pan aside. Then she places the remaining six roasted beets onto a doubled sheet of tin foil and wraps them up. "Gave yuh all the beets," she says. "We'll be switchin' tuh corn tomorrow."

She ladles macaroni and cheese into another pie pan. The cheese stretches in long strings from the baking dish. Ella finally upends the baking dish and scrapes the last of the macaroni and cheese into the pie pan. She covers both pans with tin foil and secures the foil with gum bands.

Now she turns to us with the big question. "What kinda pie yuh gonna have?" Pie is included with dinner, and the Fly Café always has at least twenty-one flavors. I am torn between lemon meringue, chocolate cream, and Dutch apple with cheddar crust. The peach pie looks good, too, but this time of year it's probably made from canned peaches. I think I'll wait until spring for peach, but the rhubarb looks fresh, and so does the cherry.

"The raspberry is the same raspberries we had in the fall," Ella says. "Froze 'em. Pies'r jus' finished, still warm. Took 'em out at five o'clock."

"I'll have the raspberry," I say decisively, "and a cup of black coffee for Dib."

Shannon doesn't even have to order her pie. Ella already knows that banana cream is the only kind she'll eat.

Everything is double-bagged in brown paper sacks and I pay $4.45 at the register. Shannon carries the bag with the pie in it and I carry the dinners and the warm rolls and Dib's coffee across the frozen tire tracks to the waiting ferry.

The wind has picked up some. The air temperature has dropped and mist has begun to rise from the river. There's a new passenger on the ferry, a man whom we do not know with a brand-new 1977 Ford Fairlane.

Dib collects the fare, two dimes from me and sixty cents from the stranger. He unties the rope and pushes the ferry away from the dock with the pole. The ferry drifts into the current. He stabs the pole into the mud at the bottom of the river and grunts with the effort of holding it steady in the stronger current on the Ohio side. Slowly, the ferry pivots around the pole until we are facing West Virginia. Dib places the pole back in the hooks on the railing.

I open the bag of rolls and a sweet yeasty smell swirls around my face. I hand out the warm rolls—one for Shannon, one for the stranger, and one for me. I give Dib his roll and coffee. He stuffs the entire roll into his mouth and drains the cup with a single swig.

Dib carries his empty cup into the pilot house. The diesel engine springs to life. He reaches out of the window and tugs twice on the rope. Shannon covers her ears as the horn blows, *broouch, broouch*.

The warm bags of food rest against my legs as I wrap one arm around the railing and one around Shannon to keep her from falling off of the boat.

The red neon sign on top of the building snaps off. The words "Fly Café—The Best Pie and We Don't Lie," dissolve into the dark river. We follow the moonlight toward home.

A Special Place

by Kathleen Stein
Los Angeles, California
2003

Surrey is one of the smallest counties in England. Evidence exists that early man inhabited certain regions at least 500,000 years ago, but it was not until 3,000 B.C., when he left recognizable earthworks in the landscape, that these early Neolithic People, with their basic skills in agriculture, flint mining, and trade, were more fully documented.

Today, one of their early tracks, subsequently known as The Pilgrims Way, is still evident along the chalk escarpment. Early remains still to be seen are "Caesar's Camp" on Wimbeldon Common (an Iron Age fort), Celtic Field on Farthing Down, and Saxon burial burrows about Coulsdon. In 1215, the Magna Carta was signed by King John at Runnymeade.

But my favorite town is Haslemere. It is very small but not too far from London. Its tiny town hall was built in 1814 and is still standing, like a tiny island in the middle of the main road.

My father's family came from here. My grandmother Kate LeGras was born and is buried there. Her mother, Maria Bicknell, had lived there all her life. I can't say if she was born there, but she is also buried there. This is where I spent most of my school holidays, in my Great Nan's cottage at the top of Shepherds Hill.

What wonderful happy memories I have treasured through all of my life. I get very nostalgic and yearn to hear a cuckoo call across an English meadow in the early morning, for Great Nan and me would be up and out to pick mushrooms in certain fields at dawn, before they got any maggot in, for she sold them to the grocery store in town.

Hindhead and the Devil's Punchbowl is close by. It's a beautiful area, especially in the autumn when all the trees turn red and golden. Then there's Blackdown Common, where Great Nan would take me to pick wild whortleberries, or "herts" as she called them. The heather is very pretty and abundant there, but it's one of the few areas in England where the poisonous puff adders and vipers are. Not many people ventured there and not once in all the times we went did we ever meet another person on the Common.

Great-grandfather Bicknell was head gardener to Alfred Lord Tennyson, the poet. I can only remember great-grandfather in his bed upstairs in the Cottage. He looked like Father Christmas with his long white beard and cheery smile. He would call me up to his room, which was very small. At the side of his single bed, on the wall, hung a large picture of several angels flying around in a blue sky. He would help me up to sit by his side on the bed. Sometimes he would just hold my hand and not say a word, but one day he pointed to the angel picture and said, "They are coming for me very soon." He seemed to be happy about it and the next time I went to visit Great Nan he was gone. She never mentioned him again. I never thought that strange at the time, for he was ninety-one years old then.

Nan's Cottage and everything in it always smelled of Sunlight Soap. It wasn't perfumed, but to this day I remember how fresh everything smelled. All my happy memories of Haslemere and Great-Gran are held together by different aromas, the heather on Blackdown Common, the blackberries at the summer's end. In the spring roaming through the fields full of cowslips, tiny yellow trumpet-like flowers with velvety sage-colored leaves, and the bluebells, the perfume was indescribable.

I often relive those golden days of my childhood and realize how fortunate I was to have lived in those lovely times, when nature was so unspoiled and beautiful.

Emigrants
&
Pioneers

*The hardest thing in life
is knowing which bridges to cross
and which to burn.*
— David Russell

A SKETCH OF THE LIFE
OF ROBERT THORNLEY

by Wilson Robert Thornley
Submitted by Janis Lapides
La Canada Flintridge, California
2004

Foreward

*Fortunately for me, my father's side of the family
are not only good at telling family stories,
but were also good about writing them down. It is to my
late Great-Uncle Wilson that I give thanks
for his diligence in writing "A Sketch of the Life of Robert
Thornley." Only a few photocopies have been made of his
hand-typed original and I am fortunate to have in my possession
one of those copies. Through it, I feel I have come to know my
Great-Great-Grandfather. Because of the length of "A Sketch of
the Life of Robert Thornley," I have submitted only Wilson's
introduction, and a portion of Chapter Five.*

— Janis Lapides

I wrote this biography chiefly with the intent to preserve for those to whom he endeared himself some of the most interesting and vital incidents in the life of my grandfather, Robert Thornley. Moreover, as I study the few facts about him which have been collected in writing, or remember his own stories, I can see much in his life and character that might well serve as ideals to be incorporated into the lives of his descendants.

To one not closely connected with him nor familiar with the history of the town which he helped to found, he will appear merely as a more or less interesting, though unimportant, type of pioneer emigrant. His experiences can perhaps be duplicated by numerous instances in the lives of other pioneers. But in the town of Smithfield [Utah], and to those who knew and loved him, he will always be an individual with a character and life of achievement worthy of their admiration and respect. For myself, I wrote not primarily of a recognition of his achievements, nor a knowledge of his character, nor a belief in his philosophy of life, but rather because of a love for a kindhearted, gentle old man who was my friend.

BANCROFT, IN HIS HISTORY OF UTAH, says: "In 1859 Seth and Robert Langton, [and] Robert and John Thornley traveled northward from Salt Lake City in search of an agricultural site. They settled within a half mile of the present town of Smithfield, Cache County. ... At the close of 1861 there were in operation a lumber mill, a molasses mill, and a tannery, and the town had been laid out in its present form."

It shall be my purpose in this chapter to clothe this bold, matter-of-fact statement of an incident in the history of Utah with grandfather's recollection of some of his experiences during this period.

After the preliminary survey of Cache Valley, Robert Thornley and Seth Langton determined to go there with their families. Langton's outfit was comparatively new, and he was in possession of a fresh yoke of oxen; so that he was anxious and ready to go immediately. Robert had a poor outfit for which he had traded his home, and his ox team was rather badly worn from the first trip to Cache Valley. He hesitated to trust himself and wife to them on such a long trip, and he also hated to put off going until another year. He decided finally to take the risks, and the two men left Salt Lake with all they owned early in October.

Langton, who had the ablest team, usually went ahead, picked out a suitable camping place, and made the camp comfortable for the night, while Grandfather with his slow team caught up later in the evening. This plan worked with great satisfaction until Robert reached what was called the sand ridge between Willard and Ogden. There was no road at that time, and the heavy sand dragging at the wagon wheels was too much for the already weakened oxen. One of the oxen fell and refused to rise. Langton was too far in advance to be of any assistance, and Robert was left in the middle of what was virtually a desert without means of moving. The situation was too serious to permit delay.

After casting about uselessly for some expedient, Robert hitched up his buckskin trowsers, shifted the yoke from the fallen ox onto his own shoulders and, with his wife pushing at the wheel, using the whip on the ox beside him, and driving the worn one which staggered on ahead, he pulled the wagon through the sand to a suitable camp. By stopping at short intervals and by almost super-human effort, they managed to drag the outfit to Calls Fort, a distance of nearly twenty miles.

Here Grandfather found a ranch apparently deserted of human beings, but on which a number of oxen were grazing. He decided to "borrow" an ox. After examining the herd, he chose one in good condition and presumably well broken since its horns were worn by the yoke. This ox he yoked with his stronger one and drove on, catching up with Langton later. During the next few days they crossed without mishap the Wellsville mountains into Wellsville. The party then made its way across country to Summit Creek, about nineteen miles northeast of Wellsville, and there camped, as Bancroft says, one-half mile from what is now the center of Smithfield.

As soon as a camp had been established so that he was reasonably sure of the safety of his property and his wife, he started back to Calls Fort with the borrowed ox. He, of course, did not know the owner; and if he had, would probably have been a little reluctant to meet him. So arriving on the same range as that from which he had taken the ox, he turned the brute loose to find its way home and returned toward the valley. On his way back, he had an experience of which he loved to tell, and which indicates at once the hardships pioneers had to bear and the hardihood they possessed which rendered it possible for them to survive.

Thinking to save time, he decided to go directly east to Summit Creek from the western divide, instead of taking the roundabout way through Wellsville. He knew that he must cross Logan River at its junction with the Bear River, but counted on using the ice for a bridge, there being thick ice on all the smaller streams he had crossed. Imagine this lonely young man as he tramped eastward over ground, which only thirty-five years before had been unknown to white men. His heart was full of hope, however, as he quickly covered the distance between the divide and the river.

When he reached the banks, however, he was chagrined to see that the current had worn away the ice in the middle of the stream so that a gap of muddy water stretched about three feet between the tapering paper-thin edges of ice. The cold was so intense that Robert was afraid of the delay should he follow the river to the fort. Even then he would probably find the same difficulty. So he determined to attempt a crossing here.

Ever resourceful, Robert cut willows from the bank, bound them into two bunches with his suspenders, and then choosing a spot which seemed narrower than any other, he began feeling his way cautiously across the gap. He depended on the willows, which he placed under each knee, to spread his weight over a sufficiently large section of ice as to prevent its cracking and letting him through. Inch by inch he worked his way over, using the willows as skis. When he reached the stretch of open water the willows bent downward, threatening at every move to precipitate him into the icy

41

stream. Robert prayed and struggled and prayed and struggled and finally, to his great relief, succeeded in worming his way across the gap. When he stood up on dry land again he discovered that his troubles were not over. His clothing up to the hips was thoroughly drenched with water and he began to shiver violently. From the river to the camp on Summit Creek, it was a life-and-death battle between the cold and his vitality. His trowsers, frozen stiff, hampered his movements and chafed his legs until they were raw; but his activity kept the warm blood moving rapidly through his body.

He finally arrived in camp, his clothes like boards but his body warm. So hardy was his constitution that the next day he was able to do his usual amount of work without apparent difficulty.

RESOURCES

Foreward to _A Sketch of the Life of Robert Thornley_, and a portion of Chapter 5, by Wilson Robert Thornley

Bancroft, Hubert Howe, _History of Utah, 1540-1886_, San Francisco: The History Company, 1889.

My Grand-Aunt, Aunty Tom

by Frank F. V. Atkinson
Canberra, Australia
2004

My grand-aunt I remember as a gentle old lady, and to grown-ups around her she was known as Tom or Tommie. To me as a child she was Aunty Tom. So you ask, "How did your grand-aunt have the name Tom? Was it her genealogical background? Or was it more likely family history?"

Aunty Tom was born in 1871, eighth of thirteen children. Her parents, Charles Sibley and Emma Lillias (née Smith), christened her Emelia Gertrude Sibley. I would not have liked calling her Gertrude or its abbreviation, or Emelia or Amelia, as she has been recorded, or Millie as shown in one family memento.

Grandparents of Aunty Tom had married in St George's Church, Bloomsbury Way, London, on 22nd June 1826, as William Sibley a carpenter, and Charity Maria Dewfall. These were my great-great-grandparents. Their firstborn was William Junior, christened at the then-new St Luke's Church in Chelsea, where Charles Dickens was married nine years later. My Sibley family sailed in the small

Hamilton in 1872, showing bridge & Sibley's mill (tall building).
Photo courtesy of Archives Office of Tasmania (Reference 30/674A)

three hundred-sixty-one-ton barque *Wanstead*, and landed at Hobart Town in late autumn on 20th May 1828, after a voyage of five months! This Australian Colony was commenced only twenty-five years previously in 1803, originally being known as Van Diemen's Land: the name given by the Dutchman Abel Tasman in 1642. William Sibley purchased horses and hauled their carts and possessions up to New Norfolk and on to Hamilton and beyond toward Bothwell, squatting at Hollow Tree Creek. Here they named their farm Cockatoo Valley and ran sheep. "Squatting" being an Australian term where a pioneer settled on Crown land, initially without government permission, until the country had been mapped. Nine years elapsed before surveyors marked out Sibley's property, enabling its purchase. William built some simple stone sheds and a cottage and later a two-story timber house with a beautifully crafted wooden staircase. Pioneering in the Tasmanian backwoods, Charity gave birth to another three children: Anne, Charles, and Eliza.

The 1830s were the height of the black wars, local aborigines being the Big River Tribe. Following the relocation of these natives,

44

their numerous dogs became feral, killing great numbers of sheep. This was also the time when the convict-built road from Hamilton deteriorated to such an extent that a landholder fenced it off and opened a separate track. On file in the Land and Surveys Department is a delightful family anecdote. A letter from Hamilton's minister describing this problem said, "the road was later reopened by Mr Sibley and his team of bullocks." Oh, what a picture one imagines.

A family legend tells that William built one of the early timber bridges over the River Clyde at Hamilton's southern end. This bridge was vital, but washed away in large floods every half-a-dozen years when heavy spring rains and melting of the snows coincided. William also took over the building of Hamilton's St Peter's Church in 1838 after the previous builder had difficulties. The 1840s saw the *banditti*, as the Tasmanian bushrangers were called, and particularly the Cash gang, raiding and robbing the Hamilton area. Laboring men were leaving the island and rushing to the settlement of Melbourne and the 1851 gold discoveries in the mainland Colony of Victoria, hence farm labor became scarce. William was given convict assistance in 1852 when he was awarded three men who were new arrivals from the convict ship *Rodney*.

Aunty Tom's grandfather was popular, being elected a town councilor; then in 1865, he was elected for his area of Cumberland in Tasmania's House of Assembly, and later again for a second term. Another interesting family note can be read in William's obituary (*The Mercury*, Hobart 14th December 1871). The parliamentary reporter wrote, amongst other things, such as William's wide circle of friends: "He was not a man of brilliant parts." While not a flattering comment, I assume that the reporter personally knew my great-great-grandfather and that his words were an honest description.

FATHER OF AUNTY TOM was Charles Sibley, born in Cockatoo Valley in 1832 and who grew up in the above-described frontier conditions, with little education apart from carpentry training from his father and very basic reading, writing, and arithmetic. Charles worked as a carpenter in Hamilton and was awarded contracts for repairing local council buildings, including the jail. In late 1850s onwards he operated the family-owned, water-driven flour mill and bakery built by Thomas & William Roadknight in 1824, and which became known as Sibley's Mill. In 1871, he was required to attend a council meeting to explain removal of material, including timber from a local Police Station: No doubt this was a carpenter's perk!

An 1878 Education Department list of children eligible to attend school shows five of the children, including Amelia. Actual attendance was another matter: Teachers were not always available, and when they were there, they wrote complaints about class attendance of fifty percent or even less. Child labor was common and children were given various jobs, or were employed by others on jobs that must be worked before school. During hops and fruit-picking seasons, classes were even emptier as families struggled to earn a little extra money. This became so serious that the Education Department eventually programmed school holidays to encompass these harvests.

AMELIA WAS A TEENAGER when her mother died and my grand-mother, second born, took care of her younger siblings. Now, to answer your question: I recall Granny telling family stories and that Aunty earned her name from being a tomboy—was there ever any doubt? A pioneering grandfather who trampled fences with his bullock team, and who "was not a man of brilliant parts"; a backwoods' father who pinched timber from a police station; a school system woefully inadequate, and too many in the family for her to be closely watched: so Amelia skipped school, rode the farm carts, climbed trees, and played with her six brothers, being a cheeky tomboy in Tasmania's backwoods.

Hence the gentle old lady who I knew in the 1940s and 1950s could have no other name but Aunty Tom.

SEARCH FOR ROOTS

by *Katherine Yamada*
Glendale, California
2002

I walked down the steeply sloped path leading to the tombstones of my husband's ancestors. Clutching a seventy-year-old picture of the three stone monuments in my hand, I wondered if they would still be there, or if they had succumbed to the salt air blowing in from the Kaminoseki Straits of the Inland Sea.

My husband, Glenn, and I were on a search for his roots, and one of our first stops was the remote village of Nerio on the very tip of Yanai Peninsula in southern Japan.

We were looking for the tombstones constructed in 1917 by Glenn's grandfather, Nobukichi Yamada. He was born in 1880 in Nerio, a tiny collection of houses clinging to the side of a mountain overlooking the straits.

The view from Nerio is an incredible one. The mountains tumble straight into the sea and the coastline is dotted with small tree-covered islands. However, farmers need room to plant crops and Nerio's steeply terraced hillsides didn't provide much land for making a living. So, when Nobukichi and his brother came of age, they left their small holdings on the hillside and came to the U.S. in response to a railroad company appeal for laborers.

Nobukichi returned to his home village in 1912. He married Tomi Kuniyuki and brought her to live in the house in which he had grown up. After fathering a son named Tadao, my husband's father, he returned to his labors in California to earn enough money to bring his wife and son to the U.S.

Four years later, he returned to Nerio to make arrangements for Tomi and Tadao to emigrate to the U.S. It was on this visit that he built the tombstone we were seeking.

Nobukichi built it in the hope that, after a few more years of hard work in California, he could return to Japan with his family. However, politics changed the course of his dream.

Prohibition and the Depression caused California land values to plunge, and immigrants like Nobukichi realized they'd never see a large return on their farming investments. Then World War II dealt the final blow. During the occupation of Japan, property owners who no longer lived within the country were forced to sell their holdings at a great loss. Nobukichi had to sell the house he'd been born in, cutting his ties to his homeland forever. Nobukichi lived out the remainder of his life on his farm in central California.

Now, some eighty years after his grandfather emigrated, Glenn and I walked down the cemetery path. As we rounded the last curve, the trio of tombstones came into view. There was Nobukichi's stone, glistening in the sun reflected off the Inland Sea. Next to it were the stones of his parents and grandparents. We stood there, reflecting on all the dreams and hardships those stones represented. Nobukichi never realized his goal of returning to Japan and being buried next to the ashes of his father and grandfather. Instead, his bones lie in Smith Mountain Cemetery in the San Joaquin Valley.

But in many ways, his dreams have been fulfilled. His eight children have become landowners of a certain stature, and many of his twenty-one grandchildren attended college in search of white collar professions. His great-grandchildren increase in number each year, with a new generation of great-great grandchildren already on the way.

His descendants adopted their new homeland with fervor and patriotism, eager to make their living in a country so rich in possibilities.

So, it was with gratitude in our hearts that we stood at Glenn's grandfather's tomb, paying tribute to a man who pursued his dream.

TOUCHING YESTERDAY

by Wanda J. Pace
Temecula, California
2002

I t was stored in a box in my linen closet until five years ago, when I first learned its intriguing pioneer history. "It" is a red-and-white quilt top made by my great-grandmother more than one hundred years ago, much like the Red Work that is popular in quilting circles today. It consists of lovely red embroidery on white squares. Flowers, vases, birds, wishing wells, and other outlines adorn forty-two squares, each trimmed in red, and sewn together with a red border around the whole. One embroidered square appears to have been made by a daughter. It is an outline of "Mother's Hand," with the date, "1893."

When I learned about my great-grandparents from a genealogical book containing a collection of old pictures and old letters dating back to Civil War days, I pulled the box from a shelf. I slowly unwrapped the souvenir and read my mother's inscription pinned to the fabric, "Jane Augusta Phillips Ames, Born 1845 Orange County, Michigan. Died 1895, Custer County, Oklahoma."

Suddenly I realized this was more than a piece of cloth, it was a piece of history. As I carefully unfolded the old fabric, I sensed a connection to the one whose hands produced this treasure and felt transported in time, and as though I were watching her work on this unique creation of yesterday.

I see her sitting by a window on an autumn afternoon, the sunlight falling over her shoulder, her dark hair streaked with silver. Afternoon is the only time she can sew. The oil lamp is not bright enough during the evening hours. Her eldest daughter, Emma, is sitting at her feet. Jane has a sewing basket and two stacks of quilt squares beside her, some finished and some still to be embroidered. She is showing Emma how to achieve this artistry. In her hand, the small needle deftly goes in and out of the material. The tiny stitches are evidence of her skill. She has been a seamstress for many years, even weaving towels for Henry Ford's mother when they lived on adjoining farms in Dearborn, Mich.

Jane and Stephen Ames met during wartime and married in 1865. They had thirteen children. Their lives were a classic story of love and devotion, tragedy and survival following the Civil War. When the eighty-acre farm in Michigan didn't prosper, they moved to Iowa. Following a great disappointment in Iowa, Stephen dreamed of moving west.

Then in 1892, the government announced a Homestead Act offering one hundred-sixty acres of land in the Oklahoma Territory to all who qualified. The lure of free land was irresistible to the poor, the courageous, the dreamer. Stephen qualified on all counts.

Stephen and Jane had more than a year to prepare. Stephen built and waterproofed the covered wagons. He chose the animals and equipment needed for the trip and a new start in Oklahoma. Although extremely limited in space, Jane decided to take a few cherished items—her diary, letters, pictures, her Bible, and the red-and-white quilt top—things she just couldn't part with. These keepsakes she wrapped in coarse muslin for protection against dirt and

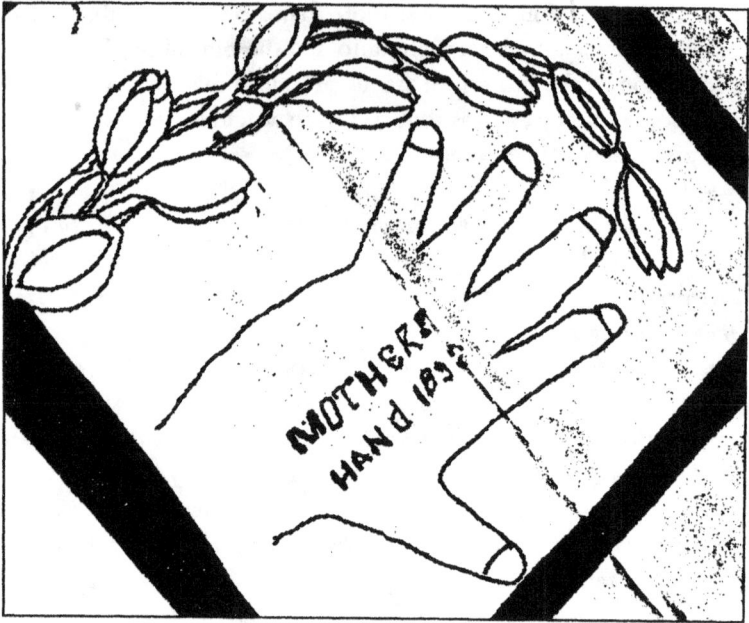

dust, and placed them at the bottom of a large trunk. Jane and Stephen sold their household goods and farm equipment and loaded the sparse necessities on two covered wagons.

Jane said a tearful goodbye to her mother, fearing she would never see her again, yet hoping that, somehow, it would be possible. Jane and Stephen Ames then embarked on the six-hundred-mile journey with six daughters, three sons, two wagons, seven horses, and their dog, Bingo. After thirty days, they arrived at Seven Oaks in Oklahoma Territory. Their temporary home was a dugout with four front windows, not uncommon at the time. Soon, Stephen left to file a homestead claim in Guthrie, where he was stranded in a bitter winter snowstorm.

While he was gone, Jane became seriously ill with pneumonia, and she died on February 14, 1895, just three months after arriving on the new frontier. When Stephen came home, neighbors met him with the dreadful news. They had done all they could to help the children. They set up a tent on the frozen ground to keep the body.

Stephen "was heartbroken, for he loved the sweet mother of his children so dearly," according to a daughter. Jane was buried in the Beck Cemetery outside of Thomas, Oklahoma. A few days after Jane died, Emma opened the trunk looking for warm clothing for her five sisters; the youngest was five years old. Jane's Bible, pictures, letters, diary, and quilt top were discovered at the bottom of the trunk, still wrapped in cloth. Emma left them there, where they remained for many years.

THE UNFINISHED QUILT TRAVELED almost 2,000 miles, from Michigan to Iowa, to Oklahoma, and, eventually, to California with my grandmother Elizabeth Roxana Ames, who was nine years old when her mother died. She kept the quilt top for more than forty years, and left it to my mother, who handed it down to me.

For many years, I didn't realize the sentimental or historical value of this treasure. Now, I know how fortunate I am to have this keepsake from the past with my great-grandmother's handiwork. I will appreciate it and care for it with the respect it deserves.

As I examine each square and lovingly place my hand on the outline of her hand, strangely, I feel as though I am touching that yesterday long ago, when Jane Augusta Phillips Ames sat in the afternoon sunlight, sewing together the whimsical squares that make up this lovely heirloom.

'NOTORIOUS STRUMPETS AND DANGEROUS GIRLS'

by D. Elwern Jones
Denbighshire, North Wales
2004

Many of my friends bemoan the fact that while researching their family history, they can find no interesting characters, not even a skeleton or two. I guess among all my many Robertses, Thomases, etc., I would have the same problem, had not my great-grandfather Robert Roberts of Llannefydd married a young lady from Henllan by the name of Ann Lunt. Her family history has provided me with many fascinating tales—and yes—I do have one skeleton in the cupboard, which I might tell you about later.

As far as I can ascertain, only two of my ancestors left these shores to settle in America. One was my six-times great-grandmother's brother, Henry Lunt, who emigrated to New England, along with three Puritan fathers, Messrs. Woodbridge, Parker, and Noyes.

The other was also named Henry. At the National Library in Aberystwyth, Wales, I had seen a reference to a Henry Lunt, Bishop

Patriarch, Cedar City, Utah. Could there possibly be any connection? In all honesty, I hoped not—because it was recorded that he had had to flee to Mexico—but I was intrigued and naturally wanted to find out more. In the local LDS Centre in Rhyl, I was surprised to see that some of my more recent ancestors had been taken through the Temple Rites of the Mormon Church by an Edward Lunt and an Edward Earl Lunt. I had no idea who they were.

Some years later, I visited Salt Lake City with a tour organized by the *Family Tree* magazine, and spent a whole fortnight researching in the world's largest genealogical library. There I found the descendancy charts for Henry the Bishop, and found among his descendants Edward Lunt, 1885, and Edward Earl Lunt, 1903. Naturally, I had to find out more.

I learned that Henry was born in Cheshire in 1824. He and his brother Thomas had invested in the gold mines in Australia. When the mines failed, Henry went to work in Birmingham, and came under the influence of the Mormons. He saved his money with the idea of going to America, and in January 1850, he left Liverpool for New Orleans, and arrived in Salt Lake City just over seven months later. He was made an Elder, then ordained, and was asked to go and work in Cedar City in Iron County.

The journey was one of great hardship—they encountered snow and high winds, only making about five or six miles a day. In some cases, the trail was so steep the men had to hold onto the wagons to keep them from tipping over. Some of the oxen were killed by wolves. Provisions had run short and they were entirely out of flour. Henry's clothes were starting to wear out, and his shoes had already worn out—he had to go to his first meeting in cloth coat, silk hat, and barefooted!

In the library catalogue, I also found Henry's hand-written diary from February 1852 to July 1853, which had been microfilmed. One entry, June 21, 1852: "Nearly all the folks in town went off to Elk Horn Springs in wagons and carriages to hold a picnic party. There were very few of us left in camp. About eleven a.m., ten Indians came to our house and seemed rather saucy. I gave them a smoke

55

and a piece of bread each." July 20: "I am this day twenty-five years of age."

In March 1852, Henry married Ellen Whittaker, the first of his four wives. Their first home was a wagon box—they only had one chair and very few tin dishes, which Ellen's mother had given them. Ellen had no children of her own, so they adopted two Indian children—a little boy called Ammon, who was given them by an old Parvan chief in return for an old rifle, a shirt, a sack of flour, and an old pair of pants—and a little girl they named Ann. Both were model children, but they died in their early youth.

Ellen stood as witness at Henry's second marriage, to Mary Ann Wilson. Ellen opened her heart and her home to Mary Ann, and taught her millinery and to knit and spin. Mary Ann and Henry had three sons and five daughters.

In April 1863, Henry took a third wife, Ann Gower—she was just nineteen years of age. She was a faithful wife and worked hard in the home. She had ten children. In 1878, Henry married again—his fourth wife was a young, distant cousin, Sarah Ann Lunt. She was to have another seven children to Henry. It appears that they all lived happily together, and Henry loved them all.

However, following the enforcement of the anti-polygamy law of the U.S. Congress in 1884, Henry, like all men who had more than one wife, had to choose among his wives and divorce all but one, or be sent to jail, or go into hiding. The first two were unthinkable, so he went into hiding. The persecution became so great that he decided to take his families and flee to Mexico. They made the hazardous journey by wagons, crossing the great Colorado River, and eventually arrived in Mexico in 1888.

It was quite exciting finding all this out, even if the relationship between this Henry and me is ever so remote. In fact, further research revealed that we only link up at my ten-times great-grandfather (also a Henry Lunt).

So, Henry wasn't the skeleton I referred to. But, that proverbial skeleton we all hope to avoid did eventually come tumbling out of the cupboard, and would not let me rest until I found out more—

and more!

It all started when I read Deidre Beddows exciting book, *Welsh Convict Women*, a study of women transported form Wales to Australia 1787-1852. The name of Alice Lunt of Denbighshire made me sit up and take notice. I just couldn't let poor Alice rest until I found out what her misdemeanour was to warrant such a harsh sentence. According to Beddows, Alice was tried at the Great Sessions in March 1824, and was transported in the ship *Henry* to Van Dieman's Land for life. And so my search was on.

The *North Wales Gazette and Weekly Advertiser* dated Thursday 15 April 1824 gave the following list of prisoners (with their sentences) when tried at the Assizes for the County of Denbigh, and held in the County Hall at Ruthin: Hugh Hughes, Alice Lunt, M. Humphreys, Elizabeth Roberts, and Jeremiah Davies, for stealing thirteen sovereigns and four half-sovereigns, the property of Edward Hughes, Llysfaen. It appears the five were taken to Ruthin Gaol for what was described as a Highway Robbery on Christmas Day 1823 (probably after some revelry on Christmas Eve).

At Alice's trial, Elinor Owen of Pentrevoelas was also transported for stealing from a dwelling house, whereas Thomas Jones of Llanelian was acquitted for the wilful murder of his father, as was Anne Hughes of Poolmouth for administering arsenic to her husband!

The majority of those transported to Van Dieman's Land had been convicted of offenses against property, rather than against persons, no matter how grave the offense committed. Offenses against property were considered capital offenses until well into the 19th Century.

Alice was taken to London (Woolwich) to await the convict ship that was to take her to Van Dieman's Land. A gig was used for the journey from Ruthin to Wrexham, then a coach proceeded the rest of the way, complete with guard.

Robert Williams, the gaoler, was paid ten pounds eighteen shillings expenses for his part in conveying convicts to Woolwich.

The ship *Henry* made only two convict runs, one in April 1823 and the next from London on 12 October 1824.

This second run was solely for female convicts, who numbered seventy-nine. The ship docked in Australia on 27 February 1825, a journey of one hundred thirty-eight days. Conditions on board ship were squalid and punishments were often brutal and frequently unjust. The sleeping quarters were dark and gloomy and utterly foul. The convicts' clothes were usually the same ones on disembarkation as had been issued when they joined the ship, so they were in tatters long before arrival at their destination.

Well, it was not until October 1994 that I was to find out what had become of Alice. It was then that I again spent two whole weeks in the genealogical library in Salt Lake City. My biggest shock at the library was when I came across a very large, very thick book naming convict women sent to Van Dieman's Land 1803-1829. My heart missed a beat—surely I wouldn't find Alice's name in that book, titled *Notorious Strumpets and Dangerous Girls*. I took a deep breath. Yes, there she was!

I learned, somewhat to my relief, that she had been married prior to her conviction—but whom had she married? Were there any children of that marriage? Of Alice's colonial experiences, I read that she was insolent and had absconded several times. I would very much like to go back yet again, just to consult that book, and make a study of the many Welsh girls featured in it. According to the book, "Alice speaks Welsh, English very little. Charlotte Davies and Jane Griffith, both Caernarvon Great Sessions, speak Welsh, English very little" All these girls, and many more besides, were accused of insolence and of disobeying orders, which may be understandable if their knowledge of English was limited. For this, they were sent to work in a factory and kept on bread and water for a week—Charlotte for fourteen days, and a few days later, had her head shaved; Jane ten days bread and water and ten days in an iron collar. Later, Jane had to sit in the stocks for three hours.

I didn't have time to record many more details. These are only a few of the Welsh girls named—the book contains the names of

1,675 transportees. Their convictions were mainly for petty thefts, such as stealing three handkerchiefs or a gown, or two shirts, or picking pockets. Those transported had been convicted of offenses against property rather than against persons, as I said. I am almost convinced that these young women were sent off to Van Dieman's Land to help build a new colony.

Alice's death is recorded, but, sadly, there is no date given or burial place, as there is in other instances.

Is that the whole story, then?

Well—no!

I have now come across the following from Denbigh Quarter Sessions: John Lunt convicted at the Denbigh Assizes by the JP at Bodelwyddan, for having run away, leaving his family chargeable to St. Asaph. John was sent to hard labour at Ruthin until the following Sessions. I also read that he was charged for neglecting his children, and for this, he was whipped several times on the Square in Denbigh. The year? Yes, 1824! The year Alice was taken to Ruthin Gaol.

So, here I go again. It is true—family history never, ever ends!

Connections

Our lives are connected
by a thousand invisible threads.
— Herman Melville

A WORTHWHILE SEARCH

by Libby Atwater,
Ventura, California
2004

My hands shook as I touched the telephone keypad, carefully inserting the ten digits that would connect me with someone I had been waiting my entire life to meet—my birth mother. Only one day earlier, on September 27, 2004, the ninety-eighth anniversary of my adoptive mother's birth, I had sent out six e-mails before lunch.

The message read:

> *I am a personal historian seeking information on Angela Scaglione, who lived in Irvington or Newark, New Jersey, in the late 1940s. I found your name through the Google search engine and thought you might help me with this project. If you have any information that might help my search, please reply via e-mail or telephone me at the number listed below. Thank you.*

Within an hour, I received a reply.

I know this person. What kind of information are you looking for? For whom and why? (signed) Jerry Scaglione.

I wrote back immediately.

Thank you for responding to my query. The reason I am seeking this information is for my own personal history. I was born in 1948, and my birth mother is listed as Angela Scaglione. I was given up for adoption shortly after my birth, and I have always wondered about my birth mother. My adoptive parents died in 1962 and 1963, when I was a teenager. I was afraid to seek my birth mother and family for many years, unsure of what I would find. However, I would really like to know my history for a number of reasons. I have had some health problems that may have biological links, and I have two grown sons who share my heredity. It would also be very nice to meet my birth family, if, and only if, they feel the same way. I hope the information I have provided will not shock or upset you. I would really appreciate your help.

The reply came back within minutes.

Yes, it is a little shocking, and I am investigating this with a few family members. I will get back to you ASAP.

After this reply, I became nervous—afraid I would not hear from Jerry again. I volunteered some additional information that I had been given about my birth. I heard nothing for the remainder of the day.

The next morning, I opened my e-mail immediately. The note from Jerry read as follows.

You are definitely a member of our family. The circumstances of

your birth are a little different from what you were told—except
for the Italian part. I am your first cousin. My father, your uncle,
will talk to his sister today and ask her if she'd like to meet you.
Please send me a phone number and the times you can be reached,
and I'll call you later. Whether or not she wants to talk to you,
you have a right to know.

I was so excited, I felt I could fly, and no one was around to share my news. My husband was in business meetings all day, and my sons and daughter-in-law were at work. I couldn't leave the house, afraid I'd miss Jerry's call, but eventually it came—at five-thirty p.m.

"You have a mother, a brother, and a sister who all want to meet you," he told me. "Unfortunately, your father died in August 2003, but the rest of your family is alive and very happy that you found them. Here are their phone numbers."

Now, here I was dialing the phone. I listened as it began to ring—once, twice, a third time—and then a woman picked up and said, "Hello."

"Is this Angela?" I asked. "I'm your daughter."

"How are you?" she replied. "I always wondered what happened to you. It's been more than fifty-six years!"

"I'm fine," I answered. "I'm really fine, thank you. I've wondered about you all my life."

"Have you had a good life?" she asked.

"I have a very good life," I said. "There have been some ups and downs along the way, but I'm doing fine."

"I'm so sorry you didn't find me sooner. Your father would have loved to meet you. He died last year. I miss him terribly."

"I'm sorry I didn't get to meet him, too. What was he like?"

"Oh, he was such a happy guy. Loved music. From the moment he got up in the morning, that radio was on. Toward the end he had problems—mini-strokes. He began to wander, and I had to lock him in the house when I went out."

We talked for quite a while, and Angela said, "This call must be costing you a lot of money."

"It's all right," I said. "I've waited too many years to make it." Before I hung up, I said, "Thank you."

"For what?" she asked.

"For giving me life," I answered. And then I began to cry.

I learned my story that night, or the parts of it that I had been seeking for a long time. My mother is now seventy-two; my brother, John, is fifty-five; and my sister, Barbara, is forty-nine. My father died in August 2003, shortly before his seventy-third birthday. I have eight nieces and nephews, and a great-niece, who was born on Labor Day. They are a warm, loving Catholic family. None of them except my mother, father, aunt, and uncle, knew about me until my e-mail arrived in my cousin Jerry's inbox.

My father's family was of German descent; my mother's was Italian. I was told that they fell in love quite young, although they had been forbidden to see each other. My mother became pregnant with me at fifteen, and did not tell her parents, afraid that her father would kill her and the young man she was secretly seeing.

On the day I was born, she didn't feel well and declined to accompany the family on an outing. Her father insisted that she go with them, and was ready to strike her, when my aunt interceded. "She's pregnant," my aunt announced, "and she's in labor. Don't you lay a hand on her. We're taking her to the hospital right now."

With that announcement, my Aunt Fran and Uncle Joe put my mother and their ten-month-old son in the car and sped away. I was born several hours later.

My mother held me for a minute, and then a nurse came and took me from her arms. "This baby is going to be adopted," she said, and whisked me away.

My aunt and uncle asked if they could raise me, but my grandfather was adamant. My birth would cause the family shame, and I was sent away.

My grandfather had a reputation for being heavy-handed and controlling, but he could not control my mother, no matter how hard he tried. The next year, she became pregnant with my brother,

John. Her parents made them get married. They had three more children. A son was stillborn, and my sister Rosemary died from congenital heart disease when she was only thirteen months old. My sister Barbara was born the following year.

I was startled to learn that I was the firstborn of five children. I'd always had firstborn tendencies, although I was the younger child in my adopted family. After I heard my story, I joked that I was the first waffle—the one you throw away.

Ironically, my birth family lives only a few miles from where I was raised. We frequented some of the same stores and amusement areas, but never met. In those days, adoption was a deep, dark secret, and unwed mothers were shamed.

If I had been born today, things might have been different. Instead, I've been reborn—and warmly welcomed back into the family of my birth.

A GREAT LEAP ACROSS THE POND

by Stephen Yung
Downey, California
2004

M any researchers have been trying to take the leap across the pond with their Chamberlain families, advancing our understanding of our family history. I found myself amidst such a leap while researching my branch of the Chamberlain clan.

Over the years, I was growing increasingly frustrated as I exhausted the traditional sources of information about Andrew Chamberlain, my great-grandfather. My search included the usual marriages and death certificates, census data, immigration records, newspaper articles, and conversations with numerous family members. For decades, my cousins had tried unsuccessfully to find Andrew's English birthplace. We knew from family, census, and death records that Andrew was born in 1824 and died on May 10, 1906, in Garden Plain, Sedgwick, Kansas. Andrew married Charity Jones on June 15, 1853, in Fayette, Macoupin County, Illinois. They had thirteen children.

Our research efforts were centered on the vital records for

Andrew. The census data, marriage, and death records gave no hint as to Andrew's birthplace. Conversations with relatives did not yield the location in England where their patriarch was born. The LDS Family History Center, *Ancestry.com*, *GENUKI.org.uk*, and other sources of information also drew a blank.

After gathering numerous photographs of the Andrew and Charity Jones Chamberlain family, I noticed there was a younger, diminutive man in some of the photos. Conversations with relatives led to the name of James Chamberlain. Research on the never-married James indicated he was in the Civil War, so I was off to the National Archives in Laguna Niguel, California. James spent fifteen years in the military, beginning in 1874. The last thirteen years of his life were at the Old Soldiers' Home in Sawtelle, Los Angeles, California. The inch of military records I received from the National Archives in Washington, D.C., in July of 2002 provided critical information. It gave James Andrew Chamberlain's birth as 1845 in Dorset, England. Civil Records at the LDS FHC indicated that the only James born in Dorset in 1845 was born on February 7, 1845. I assumed this was the correct James.

The General Registry Office in London sent me a certified copy of James's birth certificate. He was born in Sherborne, Dorset, England. His parents were Samuel and Elizabeth (Fox) Chamberlain. Samuel was born five miles north in North Cadbury, Somerset. Because of the difference in ages between Andrew Chamberlain (born in 1824) and James Andrew Chamberlain (born in 1845), I made a second assumption: that James was probably Andrew's nephew. I was off to the parish records for North Cadbury at the FHC. Bingo! I found only one set of brothers with the names of Samuel and Andrew born in North Cadbury. Their parents were Andrew (born in 1793) and Elizabeth (Hunt) Chamberlain. My assumptions proved valid.

About this time, I got in touch with Phil Chamberlain at the World Chamberlain Genealogical Society (WCGS). We discussed my recent discoveries and exchanged information. I planned a trip to go across the pond to North Cadbury for the last two weeks in March

2004 for further research. In addition to tromping through parish cemeteries, libraries, and county archives, I wrote numerous letters to Chamberlains in the area to see if I could meet and discuss the family with them. Relatives are a wonderful source of information.

I found a widow named Pat Chamberlain, who referred me to Sam Miller, the local postman-historian. Sam was quite helpful before and during the trip, providing me with a leap into a prior generation between my Andrew Chamberlain's (born in 1824) father, Andrew Chamberlain (born in 1793), and his father, Jeremiah (born in 1745). Sam turned out to be a half brother to a North Cadbury Chamberlain. When I visited Sam Miller, he gave me an old photograph of the North Cadbury house in which Andrew-1824, James-1825, Jane-1823, and Samuel-1819 were born. Based on the birth certificate of James Andrew Chamberlain, I visited his birthplace in Sherborne. My imagination went wild trying to picture conditions and life at the time of their childhood.

I spent a full five days in the Taunton Archives documenting all the Chamberlain names I could find. I found that Andrew was christened on August 17, 1823, with his sister, Jane. Parish Records seldom include birth dates. Our birth date of 1824 for Andrew was wrong. All the names of possible relatives were also noted.

With pages and pages of Chamberlain information, I returned home and spent weeks piecing them together into a family. I was successful with about 70% of the Chamberlains born in North Cadbury. Although this was a difficult task, it was made simpler by the fact that North Cadbury's population has historically been between five hundred and one thousand. The information, documentation, ancestry, and descendants have been reviewed by Sam, Cyril, Linda, and Bob, new-found cousins in England. Our Chamberlain ancestral line goes back to Richard, who was born in 1535 in North Cadbury.

EARLY THIS YEAR (2004), Phil Chamberlain asked me if I would find members of Andrew's family to participate in a single-name DNA study on the Chamberlains. I asked three American male descendants of Andrew and Charity (Jones) Chamberlain with the last name of Chamberlain to participate in a saliva test. They are descended from three different sons of Andrew. Last summer, I spoke with a descendant of James Chamberlain (born in 1825), who is the brother of Andrew (born in 1823). Hopefully, a male Chamberlain from James's line will participate in the DNA program. I also took several saliva kits to England in hopes of testing English cousins. Two English Chamberlains living near North Cadbury participated.

At this date the results of the thirty-seven-marker DNA tests indicate that two of the three U.S. cousins match descendants of Andrew Chamberlain in the U.S. Results from the English Chamberlains are a perfect thirty-seven-marker match with my Chamberlains. With my four DNA tests, each person has only one of thirty-seven markers that is different and that is a variance of one. The tests's variances were minuscule and support the relationship between the participants.

The current task is to trace them back through parish records to find where their line comes into my charts and connect with the descendants of Richard, our patriarch.

I have found that DNA testing not only validates my research, brings new cousins to light, and lays to rest some doubts that have arisen, but also helps others. It has broadened the Chamberlain relationships within my database. The combination of my research and the DNA tests give other Chamberlains a leap across the pond to their roots.

So don't get frustrated when you can't get over a wall in your research. Don't get glued to a date that may be wrong. Try a different direction or approach, or make a few assumptions that you can later prove or disprove through documents or technology like DNA. Keep trying. Eventually, you will find the key.

Tracing My African-American Ancestors

by Aaron L. Day
Long Beach, California
2000

The African-American Civil War Memorial was unveiled and dedicated in July 1998 in Washington, D.C. In August of that year, I had an opportunity to attend the Banks Family Reunion in Ohio. My family dedicated that year's reunion to my great-great-grandfather (on my mother's side of the family), Oscar Daniel Banks. He was in the Civil War, 1864, and a member of the 100th Regiment, Company I, of the Colored Volunteer Troops. This Volunteer Troop fought for the Union during the Civil War. His name is on the African-American Civil War Memorial.

Oscar Daniel Banks had three sons and two daughters, and I am a descendant of his son George Banks, who was my great-grandfather. My grandfather was also a George. I loved him dearly, and have very fond memories of him and my grandmother.

I am very proud of my great-great grandfather, and was especially thankful for the opportunity to honor him at the reunion. Over one hundred family members attended our reunion that year. That particular reunion brought us all closer together, and we encouraged families to talk to their children and tell them about their heritage. My grandson was especially proud of his name tag because it had so many "greats" on it: He is a great-great-great-great-grandson of Oscar Daniel Banks.

On September 26, 1998, the Day family members (my father's family) held a reunion at the Cleggs Chapel Baptist Church, of Timberlake, North Carolina. After the reunion, Dora M. Day-Parks (who is a cousin) and I talked about doing a research project for the Day family. After notifying other family members of our idea, we began our research.

People from every period have been curious about their family history, and we are no different. We want to know our family history because learning about our ancestors and their accomplishments will give us a sense of pride; their pioneering efforts have made many things easier for us; and most of all, our children need to know their heritage.

Working back with the U.S. census reports, I started with the year 1920, which was the latest report that was available to me for research. My father, James H. Day, was listed in the 1920 census at age eleven, and was also in the 1910 census. His father, James L. Day was traced back to the 1880 U.S. census. I found Milly Day, the mother of James L. Day, in the 1870 census with three children: Aaron, Henry, and Setta. That Aaron was my namesake.

From "Person County Marriage Bonds," I found the marriage record of my great-grandmother Milly Day. This record listed her husband, Washington, and her parents, Scott and Setta Day. In reviewing the 1870 census, I realized that Scott and Setta were listed just above Milly and her children. It was this discovery of my great-great-grandfather Scott that enabled me to continue my research back to 1820.

After searching through the entire 1820 census for Person County, North Carolina, without finding anyone by the name of

Day, I came to the recap page. You can imagine the sense of disappointment I felt while viewing the recap page. There were 2,817 white males and 2,615 white females, for a total of 5,432. There were also 1,890 male slaves and 1,804 female slaves listed, for a total of 3,694. I noticed the absence of names for the slaves. There were no slave names given, just numbers listed in columns, for males and females. I imagined that my great-great-grandfather Scott had disappeared into one of these columns, and was now one of the unnamed slaves. My first thought was that I would have to start searching through the Slave Schedules. I realized this would be a challenge, but I knew I had to try to locate him.

I did feel very fortunate that I had been able to go back one hundred eighty years, and discover so much about my ancestors in such a short period of time. Staff members at the National Archives and the Family History Center had made comments about my research success.

As I began turning the handle of the microfilm reader, I started planning my strategy and thinking about what to do next. I was ready to start rewinding the film when I noticed there was more information. I was overwhelmed with joy upon turning the reader. There, on the last page of the 1820 census, were the names of sixteen "Free Colored Persons," who were heads of households. There was a Thomas Day, a John Day, and a George Day included. Also listed were the wives and children of the sixteen households. There were a total of eighty free African-American people in Person County, North Carolina, in 1820. And out of the eighty, there were sixteen with the last name of Day.

I had mixed feelings for the next several moments. It was a very emotional experience for me. I was very happy to find the three Day family households. It was, however, very sad to think about the 3,694 slaves who were listed in this census with no names, just numbers in the male and female slave columns. I was unable to do any more research that day. I kept thinking about those unnamed slaves.

Scott would have been approximately fifteen years old in 1820, but children's names were not given in that census report. John was alone on the report, and had no children. There were check marks in the "1-14" age columns for Thomas and George, indicating that they each had sons in that age category. Now, I needed to find out if Thomas or George was my great-great-great-grandfather. The three previous reports gave me no clues.

From "Caswell County Apprentice Bonds," by the noted historian Katherine Kerr Kendall, I found court records involving Thomas and George. The records indicate that Thomas, son of Rachel Day, and George, son of Ann Day, were bound out as indentured servants to a Samuel Winstead on June 20, 1780. Thomas was three years old at the time, and George was four. I had now discovered the mothers of Thomas and George—another generation.

On August 27, 2000, my cousin Dora and I met in Durham, N.C., for the Day family reunion. Dora, my two brothers, William and Fred, and I drove into Roxboro that afternoon for the reunion.

The week before the reunion, I had driven into Raleigh to do some research at the state library and archives. I discovered a tremendous amount of information about Day ancestors, and the staff members were very helpful to me.

This was my first visit to North Carolina, and I was also anxious to do some sightseeing. One of my greatest thrills came that day as I was visiting the North Carolina Museum of History. I discovered a statue and a picture of the famed Thomas Day in front of the museum. Thomas Day was a 19th-Century African-American cabinetmaker. Some of his works were included in the exhibit, "The Past in Progress" at the museum.

During my research to see if George or Thomas was my great-great-great grandfather, I had located Thomas (the cabinetmaker) who lived in Caswell County, North Carolina. I originally mistook him for the Thomas that I was looking for, from Person County. Through court records, I found that the mothers of George and Thomas (Ann and Rachel) were possibly the sisters of a John Day. This John Day and his wife, Mourning Stewart, were the parents of Thomas Day, the cabinetmaker.

The fact that my Day ancestors were free has made it somewhat easier for me to track them through the many different types of documents that are available. There are register records, land deeds, tax records, the U.S. census reports, court records and other documents that have left a paper trail for those who are tracing free African-American ancestors.

Over the years, I have read several books and numerous articles about Thomas Day, the cabinetmaker. He was a skilled craftsman of Milton, North Carolina, and taught his apprentices the art of cabinetmaking. The Yellow Tavern (also know as Union Tavern) was known then as Thomas's workshop. He was one of the great black artisans and furniture-makers of the Deep South prior to the Civil War. He trained the slaves of wealthy whites and employed white apprentices to assist him.

Black furniture-makers were the master craftsmen among carpenters of that era. Thomas manufactured fine furniture of mahogany, walnut, rosewood, and cherry. He was known for his staircases, newel posts, and mantels. The very unusual patterns and motifs that Thomas used to highlight numerous stairways and architectural interiors made his work highly popular.

The Department of the Interior on May 15, 1975, declared the Yellow Tavern a National Historic Landmark. Examples of Thomas Day's furniture can be seen in the North Carolina State Museum. The curator of the museum told me they now have a total of forty-four Thomas Day items.

Thomas made a deal with the members of the Milton Presbyterian Church. He donated pews of walnut, yellow poplar, and pine, with gracefully curved arms to the church. In exchange, he and his family were given the privilege of sitting in the main area of the church—an area usually reserved for whites only.

The following day, I drove to Person County, and the birthplace of my father, James Day. I met several relatives, and we took a tour of Roxboro. Later in the afternoon, I drove into the town of Milton, the home of Thomas Day. It was a great experience to finally view the famous Yellow Tavern. I had seen many pictures and heard numerous stories about this landmark.

A major fire had damaged the building and restoration was in progress. The Thomas Day House/Union Tavern Restoration Inc. had just received a $250,000 matching federal grant for the restoration. Marian Thomas, president of the non-profit corporation restoring Tom Day's home and shop said: "Winning the federal 'Save America's Treasures' grant underscores the historical significance of the project, and the positive effects its restoration is having on the town of Milton and all of Caswell County."

Approximately two-hundred people attended our family reunion that Sunday. I was able to meet a lot of relatives; some I have known for years and others that I met that day. We passed a sign-in sheet around for names, addresses, and telephone numbers, which I added to my computer database. A number of the younger generations were very interested in the family charts that I showed, and wanted to learn more about genealogy and our ancestors.

During the coming years, I will keep in touch with these young people, and encourage their interest in genealogy. To spark their curiosity and maintain that interest, I will send family charts and group sheets to them that include their immediate families, and ask if they will help me to keep the charts updated. I will also make sure they receive a list of all family members, so they will be able to keep in touch. Finally, I will guide them through the research process, so they will learn first-hand how it is done.

My trip to North Carolina was everything that I had hoped it would be: sightseeing, researching, and meeting family and friends. I had only one disappointment: I was still unable to determine my great-great grandfather Scott's father: Thomas or George. When I eventually discover his identity, then I will know if Ann or Rachel is my great-great-great-great-grandmother.

Through court records from the state of Virginia, I have been able to locate three generations beyond Ann and Rachel. Hopefully, by our next reunion, I will have been able to verify this information so I can present it to the family. My oldest brother, William, is a great-grandfather himself, so we would then have thirteen generations of Days on record.

The August 1998 Banks family reunion honoring my great-great-grandfather, Oscar Daniel Banks, changed my life tremendously. I now realize the importance of preserving family histories for future generations. With other family members (Bankses and Days) I am now doing my part to learn about our ancestors. This information will be passed on to our descendants so that they will know their heritage.

THE BLUE FOLDER

by Mary Jane Battaglia
Placerville, California
2003

"Why are you packing that?" asked Batt, referring to my blue folder labeled "BATTAGLIA." (My husband's parents lovingly named him "Angelo," after his paternal grandfather, but his nickname is "Batt," and that's what I call him.)

"I'm packing this," I replied, tucking the folder into the bottom of my bag, "because it contains all your father could remember about his family. Since we'll be in Sicily for part of this trip, we're going to look for your cousins!"

And that's just what we did.

It was a sunny afternoon when we sneaked away from our Italian Tour Group in Palermo to take the bus to nearby San Lorenzo. It was in this small village that Batt's father, Guiseppi, was born some ninety years earlier. His much-older brother, Raffaelo, had raised him there after their parents died. Shortly before he reached fifteen, Guiseppi left for the U.S. and never looked back.

When the bus dropped us off in the Palazzo del San Lorenzo,

we looked around in dismay. This was no "small village," as described by my father-in-law! The near-empty Palazzo was surrounded by four-story apartment buildings. All windows were shuttered, doors closed. However, off at one side was a vegetable stand, around which were clustered the only visible inhabitants.

"Go ask," I said, as I pushed Batt toward the group, grateful that he had learned Italian as a child. (Smiling in English is my only linguistic accomplishment.)

In his halting Italian, Batt asked if anyone knew of a family named "Battaglia," or perhaps descendants of Raffaelo Battaglia. The vendor and his customers cautiously conferred and finally one elderly man pointed up the street.

"One block, then turn left."

With this encouragement, we followed directions and went up one block. When we turned left, however, we stared in shock. That street stretched long—lined on both sides with multi-story apartment buildings—all totally shuttered, closed, inhospitable! Not a soul in sight! The friendly door-to-door genealogical search I'd envisioned was out of the question.

While we stood debating what to do next, a car pulled up, parking nearby. As the driver left his car, I pushed Batt to "Go ask." Fortunately, the young man knew the name *Battaglia*. Unfortunately, all he knew about it was that someone of that name had recently died. However, he did believe that a son of the family lived somewhere near, back along the route we had just taken.

"*Grazie!*"

As we retraced our steps, we passed a group of teenage mechanics working on a garaged car. "Go ask!" I said, as I shoved Batt over into their midst. The boys listened, put their heads together and considered. Finally, one youngster spoke up to say that he actually knew the family. Gesturing for us to follow, he led the way to a nearby building, climbed some stairs, and rang the bell.

The voice responding on the intercom was not friendly. One had to be careful, the youngster explained to us, as he tried to convince the voice that we really were "family," and that we came from

California. The voice was unimpressed. As the boy continued to plead our case, I pulled out my blue folder. If the voice wanted proof, I had it. With the youngster translating, I read off the names of Guiseppi's parents, his brothers, sisters, and cousins. That did it. We were buzzed in.

It was family reunion time. The voice on the intercom belonged to Salvadore, who was actually a grandson of my father-in-law's older brother, Raffaelo. We were made welcome, met the rest of his family, and surprise! There was a son named Angelo. Later, Salvadore drove us to meet the family of his brother, Paulo, and their mother, the recently bereaved widow of their father, Raffaelo Battaglia II.

Paulo's family greeted us warmly, and it was no surprise that one of his sons was "Angelo." Waves of happy Italian chatter rolled right over me while Batt and his new-found cousins got acquainted. We learned that Batt's father, Guiseppi, never wrote back once he left; consequently, his Sicilian family knew nothing about what had happened to him. We all shared wine and goodies, as nearly eighty years were being bridged in one afternoon.

When Paulo learned of my blue folder, he disappeared, to return with his own folder. We pulled our chairs to another table and had a wonderful time. I spoke no Italian and he spoke no English, but we had no trouble communicating. Ours was a common language—genealogy. We shared pictures, drew family charts, and spent the remainder of the afternoon scribbling away names, dates, and places. Such a satisfying experience.

"See," I chortled to Batt as we returned on the bus to Palermo. "We really did find your cousins. Being prepared paid off."

However, as I patted my blue folder, I had to acknowledge another factor involved—dumb luck. That's one genealogical resource not to be underestimated!

Bringing
Research
to Life

There was never yet an uninteresting life.
Such a thing is an impossibility.
Inside of the dullest exterior
there is a drama, a comedy, and a tragedy.
— Mark Twain

IMAGINING SAM BURGESS

by Leslie Prpich
Victoria, B.C., Canada
2003

In his history of "The Common People of Great Britain," J. F. C. Harrison spells out plainly what all family historians eventually come to understand: No matter how curious, sympathetic, or imaginative we are, we will never be able to recreate more than a fragment of the experiences and sentiments of our working-class ancestors.[1]

Don Gayton, when he attempts to bring his great-grandfather Thomas Gayton to life, writes that lives which were largely undocumented "can be expanded by inferential research, but far more substantially by a kind of geographically centered imagination."[2]

It is this imagination the family historian learns to develop. We carefully research the skeletal facts of a life—the baptismal record; the census entry; if we are lucky, the will—and then we immerse ourselves in the local history. Once we have some knowledge of the place and the times in which our ancestors lived, the bare-bones facts of their lives take on new meaning. Many times we are able to conclude, "given this detail and that piece of local history, almost certainly this was a reality for my ancestor."

I experienced just such a moment of clarity the day George Burgess' death certificate came in the mail. Knowing what I did about George's life and times, I could vividly imagine what his death would have meant to his family—especially to his young son Sam.

Sam Burgess was born in 1838 in Longton, Staffordshire, the southernmost and the roughest of six towns in the English Midlands known collectively as the Potteries. The locals called Longton "Neck End"; Robert Slaney, the health commissioner who surveyed the area in 1845, called it "a rude scattered hamlet without form, a chaos of unarranged mud huts."[3]

There were two main jobs in the Potteries of the 1840s: making "pots" (which weren't pots at all, but dishes) and mining coal (to fuel the ovens where the pots were fired). Sam's father, George, was a mining engineer in the coal fields east of Longton. He married Hannah Wilshaw after his first wife died and became a father to her three illegitimate children, Cicely, William, and Priscilla. Sam was born a year and a half later, followed by Joseph and George at two-year intervals.

LIFE IN THE STAFFORDSHIRE coalfields was unsettled and grim. Most mine jobs didn't last long and the family moved house often. After a devastating miners' strike in 1842, George was hired on at the Mossfield Colliery in Adderley Green.[4] For a time, the family's future must have seemed at least somewhat secure. Then, on April 16, 1844, George Burgess fell down a coal pit and died. In an instant, Hannah was the single mother of six. Childhood was a luxury she could not afford. Young Sam would have to start earning wages. He was six years old.

In the Potteries of the 1840s, thousands of children worked in the potbanks. The ones as young as Sam were hired as jigger-turners, dipper's helpers, and mould-runners. When Samuel Scriven submitted his "Report on Child Employment in the Staffordshire Potteries" to the House of Commons in 1842, he concluded that the youngest children in the potbanks lived a life that was little removed from slavery.[5] The testimony of the children he interviewed reveals what life was like for a boy like Sam: *"I run moulds for William Bentley, have been at work five years. I never get a bit of play. I would rather work ten hours a day than fifteen, should not care then if I had less wages a good sight. I should go to school then and have a bit of time for play."* [6]

Potters' jobs were highly specialized: A plate-maker, for example, made nothing but plates. From six in the morning until six at night, he hunched over his "whirler" making plates. This wasn't art, it was mass production. A good maker could turn out nine hundred plates in a day.

The whirler was part of a jigger, a machine that consisted of two iron frames with a spindle in each: a driving spindle, attached to an iron belt pulley and a driven spindle, which turned the jigger head, or the whirler. The jig was attached to a moveable arm which the maker would lower and raise as he worked. He made his own jigs from clay and fired them; a plate jig measured about three inches across the top and was curved on the bottom, with a small, rounded notch cut into the curve. The machine was powered by a large vertical wheel, connected to the driving spindle by an endless rope.

The maker needed both hands free to throw a plate and shape it on the whirler, so he'd hire a boy like Sam to turn the wheel. That boy was a jigger-turner. *"I turn jigger for William Wilcox, used to run moulds. Come to work at six [in the morning] and leave at eight or half-past [in the evening]. I cannot read, I cannot write. I get two shillings a week and am always in regular work."* [7]

From a mound of wedged clay beside the jigger, the maker would cut off a lump with a wire and roll it quickly between wet hands, pressing it flat as he rolled. He pounded this "bat" on a board until one side was smooth and then he threw it, smooth side down, onto a convex plaster mould attached to the whirler. As the clay spun around on the whirler, the maker coaxed it out gently with the ball of his hand from the center toward the edges. Once it covered the mould completely, he smoothed the surface with a wet knife and cut off any overhanging clay by holding a wire against the edge of the mould as it spun. Then, he pulled the jigger arm toward him with his right hand and held it steady with his left while the notch in the jig shaped the plate's foot-ring and its curve defined the rim.

At this point, he needed a runner. He couldn't make nine-hundred plates in a day if he had to run each to the stove room. He would lift the mould off the whirler and pass it to a boy like Sam, who ran with it as quickly as he could to the stove—this was a room within a room, four or five yards square, with floor-to-ceiling shelves on all its walls and steps that could be moved along as needed. In the centre of the room was a cast-iron stove, blazing hot. The runner's job was to set the mould on a shelf, tip it forward carefully until the plate slipped off toward his hand, lean the plate against the wall, and leave it there to dry for about ten minutes while he ran the empty mould back to the maker. Once a plate was partially dry, he returned it to the maker, who slurried its back with a sponge and reapplied the jig. This process gave the plate a crisp finish that couldn't be achieved the first time because the clay was too soft.

Imagine our boy: Back and forth he would run. The faster the maker, the faster the boy had to sprint. The stove room was stifling hot and the only light was the glow of the stove. The maker was paid by the piece and only for those "good from oven." Breaking a plate was a serious matter, as two young boys told Scriven: *"William Bentley licks me sometimes with his fist, he has knocked me the other side of the pot-stove for being so long at breakfast." "I run moulds for my father; he flogs me sometimes, if I let go a mould or break a saucer."* [8]

Every half hour, the running would halt while the plate-maker shaped the next set of bats and the mould-runner wedged clay. Outside in the yard, a boy no bigger than Sam began with a block of clay about half his body weight and sliced it in two with a wire. He lifted one half above his head and slammed it down hard against the other, using all the strength he could muster, to drive the air out of the clay. Then he'd lift the other half and slam it down hard against the first.[9] Lift, slam, repeat, until the clay was the consistency of putty and the maker was ready to throw the next set of bats. *"I get meal and water for breakfast, and tatoes for dinner, sometimes a bit of bacon. I don't get enough. I could always eat more if I had it."* [10]

In winter, the temperature outside might reach twenty degrees below freezing while the temperature in the stove room ranged between one hundred and one hundred and twenty degrees. Samuel Scriven reported seeing boys running back and forth between the stove and the yard, barefoot and sweating, without jackets and often without shirts. "The results of such transitions are soon realized," he wrote. "Many die of consumption, asthma, and acute inflammations."[11]

Adult potters were no better off. Dr. J. T. Arledge, senior physician of the North Staffordshire Infirmary, said in 1863 that "the potters as a class, both men and women, represent a degenerated population. . . . They are, as a rule, stunted in growth, ill-shaped, and frequently ill-formed in the chest; they become prematurely old, and are certainly short-lived. . . ."[12]

Sam may have fared better than most. By 1851, at the age of fourteen, he had progressed to the job of warehouse boy; he likely began an apprenticeship very soon after. Typically, youths in the potbanks served a five- to seven-year apprenticeship. During that time, they did the work of an adult, often for wages that were lower than a child's.

An apprentice might earn two shillings a week; in consideration of getting no learning, a child not yet apprenticed might expect two shillings and ninepence. Once his apprenticeship was complete, a man's wages could jump to twelve shillings.[13]

My great-great-grandfather Sam Burgess learned to make bowls. Until he died of a stroke in 1899, he hunched over a "whirler" twelve hours a day, six days a week, and made bowls. He married and raised nine children and did his best to keep them out of the potbanks.

Sam was solid, a man you could count on.

From the age of six.

REFERENCES

1. J. F. C. Harrison, <u>The Common People of Great Britain: A History from the Norman Conquest to the Present</u>, Bloomington, Indiana University Press, 1985, p. 14.

2. Don Gayton, "A Schooner in Memory." In Lynne Van Luven, ed., <u>Going Some Place: Creative Non-Fiction Across Canada</u>, Regina, Coteau Books, 2000, p. 237.

3. Unknown source via Pamela Cotton, 1999.

4. There is no proof that George Burgess worked at the Mossfield Colliery, but in light of the information on his death certificate, this was the most likely place of employment.

5. Samuel Scriven, <u>Report on Child Employment in the Staffordshire Potteries</u>, 1842, published online at http://www.netcentral.co.uk/steveb/history/scriven_index.htm, downloaded 30 Dec 2002.

6. Excerpted from evidence collected at the Scriven enquiry, 1842, published online at http://www.netcentral.co.uk/steveb/history/scriven_index.htm, downloaded 30 Dec 2002.

7. ibid.

8. ibid.

9. The descriptions of the pottery-making process are derived from a number of sources, including Charles Shaw, <u>When I Was a Child</u>, (1903, reprinted by Churnet Valley Books, 1998); Arnold Bennett, <u>Clayhanger</u>, (1910, reprinted by Methuen & Co., 1952); and Charles Counts, <u>Pottery Workshop: a study in the making of pottery from idea to finished form</u>, New York, Macmillan, 1973.

10. Excerpted from evidence collected at the Scriven enquiry, 1842, published online at http://www.netcentral.co.uk/steveb/history/ scriven_index.htm, downloaded 30 Dec 2002.

11. Scriven, 1842.

12. <u>First Report of the Children's Employment Commission</u> 13 June, 1863. Published online at http://www.socsci.mcmaster.ca/~econ/ugcm/3ll3/ marx/cap1/ chap10, downloaded 30 Dec 2002.

13. Leonard Whiter, <u>Spode: A History of the Family, Factory and Wares from 1733 to 1833</u>. London, Barrie and Jenkins, 1970, p. 4.

My 111 Years
in a Danish Village

by Vicki Renfroe
Alvin, Texas
2002

rowing up, my mother's favorite stories involved her father and his parents. I remember clearly how proud she was to tell me that even though her father was born in America, he was full-blood Danish because both his parents were born in Denmark. And, though in some part of the country it may not seem like much to be of Nordic descent, this was definitely "different" in Texas.

After I began researching my family history, my aunts and uncles all wanted me to trace their Danish line and "see if we're descended from royalty." My Aunt Evelyn even volunteered to drive me to Eagle Lake, Texas, to interview the remaining siblings in order to get information about their parents' Danish birthplaces.

From elderly great-uncles who spoke with a faint accent (despite the fact they were all born in Jamestown, Kansas), I was given the village names of "Sorby" and "Shala."

"Sorby" turned out to actually be "Sorbymagle." With help from a local genealogist in Kansas and the International Genealogical Index (IGI), my Gertson line soon was traced across the Atlantic, through Sorbymagle and to Gimlinge. I was amazed at how often people moved around—my Geertsens (as they were known in the old country) seemed to be made up of a long line of wandering men. I smiled as I read the *afganliste* ("moving-in list") and the *tilgangliste* ("moving out list") kept by the priests. My ancestors' names appeared frequently. I was reminded of my grandfather, their descendant, who spent his life as an oil field roughneck and itinerant farmer. Even when he came to visit us when I was a kid, he never would stay very long.

"So that's where he got it from," I thought.

Researching my Mortensen line proved much more difficult. There was no town in Denmark named "Shala." I spent years trying to locate this village, which I eventually decided must have disappeared into history. Trail after trail brought me up short. I found Geertsen immigration records, but no Mortensen. I found my original immigrant ancestor, Peder Geertsen, in the IGI, but there was no Hans Mortensen. My Kansas connection found declarations of intent and naturalization papers for Peder and Karen Geertsen, but nothing on Karen Mortensen or her daughter, Elsie.

Chris Gertson, the son of Peter and Carrie Gertson of Jamestown, Kansas, married Elsie Mortenson, the daughter of the widow Karen Mortensen, in 1887, shortly after Elsie arrived on American soil. For twenty years, I worked on the Geertsen-Mortensen line from its beginnings in Kansas farmlands through its removal to Texas rice country. They had ten children scattered all about the country and I was kept busy for a number of years. But the information was left to gather dust as I worked on my father's line, got married, and began to raise a family.

Then one day, after being asked to volunteer in our local Family History Center, I decided to write one of my mom's cousins, with whom I had once corresponded. She no longer lived at the address, but one of her daughters did. Imagine my surprise when this relative wrote back and said that with the help of some Family History Center volunteers in Columbus, Texas, she had finally found Elsie's birthplace in Denmark! "Shala" had actually been "Skals." The worker had helped her order a Danish church film and she had found Hans Mortensen, but the language barrier proved too much for the both of them, and so she had retreated. She sent me the film number and I immediately ordered it.

My overwhelming excitement turned to dismay. I not only found myself staring at a very foreign language, indeed, but one that was written in a scrawling, archaic handwriting style on unlined paper. With the help of a guide printed by the The Church of Jesus Christ of Latter-day Saints (LDA), I deciphered important words like baptism (*daaben*), marriage (*viede*), and death (*dode*). But the old Germanic letters did not even resemble our modern-day American alphabet.

I ended up discouraged. I just put the film back in the box and returned it to Salt Lake City. I decided there was nothing more I could do but hire a professional genealogist. Since that was financially out of the question, I decided that my Mortensen line was trapped in a language barrier.

But I found myself thinking about the film again and again.

One day, I thought, "You've studied French, Spanish, and Latin and done well in all of them. Why would Danish be any different?" So I reordered the film.

Upon its arrival, I sat in front of a microfilm reader with wide eyes thinking, "Right, I'm going to translate this almost three-hundred-year-old Danish Evangelical Church record sprinkled with Latin, written in the Germanic style by a priest who had little, if any, control over his feather-quill pen."

I put the film away again.

But I kept thinking about it.

Then one day, I made a decision. I used the reader/ printer and made a hard copy of the records my cousin had cited. I studied them, comparing lettering I knew from the more-recent Danish records I had found. I picked out names I knew and studied how the letters were made. I got the film out and studied it more and found that the priest had divided the record up into baptisms, engagements, marriages, and burials. Since these were the ordinances in which he participated, they were the events that were recorded in the days before government mandated forms.

Sometimes, I'd figure out that I was reading a letter wrong: that what I thought was a capital "d" was actually a lower-case "a" (names were not always capitalized).

Eccentricities became apparent. I could tell when priests were replaced, by the variation in handwriting styles. Different priests included different information. Some of the priests were so male chauvinist that they not only didn't include the mothers' names in the birth records, but they left out the woman's name in the engagement and marriage list. This made it difficult to match husbands and wives. I shouted with joy when a priest named Andreas Woldicke took over the records. Bless his heart, he included the mothers' names in the birth records. I was sad to see him go.

Name spelling seemed to have been capricious. I was amazed to find one priest spelling the name "Therkeld" as "Terkel" or "Therkil," all in the same record.

As I traced my Mortensen line back to 1701, when the records began in Skals, I realized that, unlike the Geertsens, the Mortensens had been a stay-put people. Elsie's parents had married in the same town that they had been born in, where their parents had been married and born, and so on for generation before generation. As I journeyed backward, family lines crossed and joined until I had so many names that I was confused.

Then this wild and crazy idea popped into my head: "There are thousands, if not millions, of descendants from these people. So, because you are now able to read the record, you should transcribe it for others to use."

"No way," I told myself. "I've got four children, the youngest of whom is five months. How could I possibly have the time to compile these records?"

Well, from somewhere, the energy came. I stayed up entire

nights writing in a composition book and then retyping onto my computer marriage after marriage, engagement after engagement, christening after christening, burial after burial. When I'd finally go to bed, I could see Danish writing on the ceiling. I dreamed of villages full of farmers and sheepherders working out their daily existence.

I traced entire families through one hundred eleven years of records. I followed as some families lost child after child not long after birth. I cried as I realized that some women buried all their children and died alone. I marveled that Brigitte Therkeldsdatter had given birth to sixteen children and been able to watch all of them reach maturity. I became dismayed as Christine Sorensen gave birth to a daughter out of wedlock, only to see that daughter and Christine's granddaughter do the same. I watched as *sangfroid* (literally translated, it means "illegal bed") children were raised by grandparents, never living with their own parents, even in the instances when their parents eventually married.

I ordered census records and found family groups. I discovered the illegitimate children farmed out at early ages to work on the large sheep ranch in the area. I empathized with these exiles, as I realized that their counterparts who were fortunate enough to have been born after marriage were allowed to become apprentices to blacksmiths, shoemakers, weavers, barrel makers, etc.,

It took six months to transcribe and compile the records into WordPerfect and Personal Ancestral File programs. Many times, my kids would wake up for school and ask me what time I had gotten up. Their mouths would fall open as I would tell them that I had never been to sleep. They couldn't believe that I stayed in such a good mood with so little sleep. But the villagers of Skals would not leave me alone until I was finished.

I copied the pages, organized them, and used a coil binder to put them together. I sent a copy to the new Danish Immigrant Museum in Indiana and the Family History Library in Salt Lake City. Since then, I have had libraries order copies.

And, then, I finally got some sleep.

Sometimes I marvel that I ever finished.

Through it all, I gave birth to a fifth child, moved into a new house, was put in charge of the Alvin Family History Center, and, in general, was able to keep my home and family running smoothly. Thank goodness for a patient husband who has never begrudged me my obsession with genealogy.

I can't imagine ever tackling a project like that again. But I get a wonderful satisfaction from remembering the one hundred eleven years that I spent in a Danish village back in 1993.

A MINOR BATTLE
OF THE REVOLUTIONARY WAR

by Jean Chapman Snow
Sherman Oaks, California
2002

I f April is the cruelest month, it is especially so in Great
Barrington, Massachusetts, where spring winds may be bitter
and cold. It might even have snowed on April 21, 1775, as thir-
teen-year-old Abner Pier (rhymes with fire) watched his seventeen-
year-old brother, Solomon, march off with the Berkshire County
Minute Men. Abner was my great-great-great-grandfather.

I've often wondered how he must have felt. Was he afraid for
Solomon? Excited? Impatient to be old enough to march with
them? Was it the appeal of carrying a musket or rifle? The appeal of
a uniform, though volunteers had few? But uniforms, muskets or
no, there were doubtless stirring drum beats urging the militia on its
way to the Revolutionary War.

The next year, in July, Abner watched his father, Thomas, leave
for twenty days' service. In 1777, Thomas left again for two months.
Abner must have listened eagerly to the tales that Thomas and twen-

ty-three-year-old brother Levi[1] brought back from their services[2] in the New York Highlands, Fort Edward, and Bennington, Vermont.

Brother Solomon was the first of the Pier family to enroll with the Berkshire County Minute Men in response to the Battle of Lexington (the alarm of April 19, 1775). The name Minute Men derives from the rag-tag of colonials who enlisted at a minute's notice for short periods and/or specific sorties. They were not regular Continental Army, but farmers, shoemakers, and other ordinary folk.

Berkshire history has it that news of the Battle of Lexington arrived in the county "on the 20th about noon," and the next morning at sunrise Colonel Patterson's regiment of Great Barrington Minute Men, completely equipped in arms and generally in uniform, was on its way[3]. The distance from Lexington to Great Barrington, where my Piers had lived since 1732, was more than seventy miles. How did word fly so quickly that two days later the Minute Men could march to support the colonies? Nevertheless, march on the 21st they did.

News had been borne by fleet horsemen town to town and quickly disseminated in every direction. The town of Great Barrington lay on "The Great Road from Boston to Albany," its western edge about three miles from the New York border, its southern edge eight miles from Connecticut. Thus, as early as the French and Indian Wars, the "Great Road" had been an important military thoroughfare. Large bodies of soldiers had often billeted upon Great Barrington's townspeople and collected stores from them[4].

The Minute Men were ready, for from 1768 on, there had been turmoil in Berkshire County. The Stamp Act of 1765 (though repealed in 1776) had aroused the colonists and most, except for the few Tories, sympathized with the oppressed citizens of Boston.

By October 1768, British troops had arrived in Boston to enforce customs laws. There followed in March 1770, the "Boston Massacre," and in 1773, the "Boston Tea Party" with its three-hundred-twenty-four crates of tea flavoring Boston Harbor.

"Denunciations were heard from the pulpit . . . frequently directed against the aggressive measures of the British Ministry . . ."[5] A day of fasting and prayer was appointed, and a "League and Covenant" prepared for the non-importation, purchase, or consumption of any goods, wares, or merchandise from Great Britain after the first day of October 1774[6].

The citizens of Great Barrington were so stirred up that they imprisoned a Tory magistrate. In anticipation of impending hostilities, two regiments of men were raised during the autumn and winter of 1774. Surely Abner had listened to the townspeople's discussions and observed what was happening. How could Abner not be aroused by this patriotic fervor?

He was. Sixteen at last, he enrolled in 1779, and marched to New Haven, Connecticut, to serve one month and nine days with four-and-one-half-days travel included[7]. He next entered service June 27, 1780, for eight days to sustain the fort at West Point.

His last service was in a regiment raised July 18, 1780, to reinforce the Continental Army for three months. As a private with Colonel John Brown's regiment, he was sent to Stone Arabia in the Palatine area of New York's Mohawk Valley to fight the "savage White Sachem [Sir John Johnson] and his murderous horde of Indians and Tories, from Canada."[8] This sortie would end in disaster for Brown's men.

Mohawk Indian Chief Joseph Brant (Thayendanegea) and his troops had been sweeping up the Susquehanna River Valley to the Mohawk River, plundering farms, burning crops and houses, killing or driving off cattle and horses, murdering or taking prisoners of all they met. Even resident Tories complained of Brant's depredations.

On October 19, 1780, Brant's and Colonel Brown's forces met. Brown's one-hundred-fifty men, outnumbered ten to one, had not received their promised support from General Robert Van Rensselaer—"so unpardonably slow," says the *History of Montgomery and Fulton Counties*[9] as he was dining with Governor Clinton at Fort Plain, that the battle was a debacle. Brown was killed and his forces cut to pieces.

Later, General Van Rensselaer was universally censured for his mismanagement of this expedition, "especially his shameful negligence in allowing Stone Arabia to be desolated in his presence" by holding his forces back, allowing an enemy on the point of surrender to escape merely defeated when it might have been annihilated.[10]

History of Montgomery and Fulton Counties states that Brown was killed in the Battle of Stone Arabia on his birthday, October 19.[11] The memorial stone erected by his son reads

In memory of Col. John Brown
who was killed in battle on the 19th of Oct., 1780
at Palatine, in the County of Montgomery,
Æ 36

And Abner? One of Brant's Indians took Abner prisoner until Brant discovered him and ordered the Indian to kill him. The Indian then struck Abner with a tomahawk, shot, and scalped him. "Life was discovered by a Tory, who shot Abner again, saying 'that d-d Yankee isn't dead!' " says Shaw's *History of Cooperstown.*[12]

Another account says "Abner Pier, son of Thomas Pier . . . was taken prisoner by the Indians in the same battle. One of Pier's captors struck him on the head with a tomahawk, took off his scalp, and, as he lay helpless on the ground, shot him, inflicting several bullet wounds. Pier was then left for dead, but recovered strength sufficient to crawl to a hayrick near by, where he lay on the straw through the night and was found the next day by his comrades. He was removed and properly cared for, and, although terribly mutilated, recovered from his wounds. Mr. Pier afterwards received a pension, and for several years resided in South Egremont (Great Barrington) engaged in his occupation of shoemaking."[13]

The battle scene comes to life—Colonel Brown marching to the attack, expecting the promised support from General Van Rensselaer. Without that large army, Colonel Brown and forty of his men were killed. Stone Arabia was left in ruins by Brant and his men, and Abner, a month shy of his eighteenth birthday, left for dead.

I often wonder if Abner felt abandoned during that long night as he lay on the straw. If he had enrolled with dreams of glory, they must have vanished in the pain of his wounds.

I wonder, also, did he and Lucy Stevens, whom he married three years later, have an "understanding" before he'd left for the war? Did he dream about her during that lonely night? And I've pondered how and when Abner could have been returned to Great Barrington.

Stone Arabia (called the Battle of Klock's Field in some histories) was a minor battle in the Revolutionary War. There were neither television journalists, nor camcorders to record details, so it has taken much research to find the above. Thus, a recent discovery delighted me.

The *History of Schenectady* reports that some Schenectady militia were "detailed as guards and batteaumen to bring by boat to Schenectady those of Colonel Brown's soldiers who had sustained injuries that their wounds might here be dressed under the direction of Dr. Dirk Van Ingen."[14]

So Abner was taken up and cared for. He survived to marry Lucy and leave a family of nine children, the last of whom was born four months after Abner's death on Christmas Eve 1810. Abner and his family knew both joys and sorrows, as do we all, but for now, the rest of his tale must remain untold.

REFERENCES

1. Levi is not listed in Massachusetts Soldiers and Sailors of the Revolutionary War *(Boston, Secretary of the Commonwealth, 1896), but see Joseph Pierre,* The Descendants of Thomas Pier *(Bowie, MD, Heritage Books, Inc., 1995), p. 6.*

2. Pier, op. cit.,p. 16

3. Charles J. Taylor, History of Great Barrington, (Berkshire County) Massachusetts *(Great Barrington, Mass, 1882), p. 232.*

4. Taylor, op. cit., p. 136.

5. Taylor, op. cit., p. 225.

6. *Taylor, op. cit., p. 231.*

7. _Muster and Pay Roll Records at Archives of the Commonwealth of Massachusetts_, *Columbia Point, 220 Morrissey Blvd., Boston, Mass. 02125. Massachusetts Archives, Boston, Mass.*

8. *Spafford, Horatio G.,* _Gazetteer of the State of New-York_, *(Interlaken, N.Y., 1981 reprint of the original 1824 edition), p. 399.*

9. *Spafford, op. cit., p. 399, Palatine*

10. _____, _History of Montgomery and Fulton Counties_, *N.Y., 1878, (Interlaken, N.Y., reprint by Heart of the Lakes Publishing, 1981), p. 154.*

11. _____, _History of Montgomery and Fulton Counties_, *op. cit., p. 55.*

12. *Shaw, S. M., Editor,* _A Centennial Offering, Being a Brief History of Cooperstown_, *(Cooperstown, N.Y., Freeman's Journal Press, 1886) p. 220, and Taylor, op. cit., p. 261.*

13. *Taylor, op. cit., p. 261.*

14. _Pension Office Records_, *Nicholas R. Bovie, S 12275 and Henry H. Peek, W 9219, given in Willis T. Hanson, Jr.* _A History of Schenectady During the Revolution_, *(N.Y., 1916) from the Website http://www.bvma.org/tryon4history.html.*

Seeking Truth and Balance

by Andrea Butler-Ramsey
Bronx, New York
2003

Historians over the years had maintained that because of the institution of slavery, people of the African Diaspora had no traceable roots. I believe that we still might be holding on to that notion, were it not for writer Alex Haley and his book, *Roots*. Based on oral history, he traced his family lineage back to the village of Juffure, Gambia, West Africa. Haley illuminated the dark path through the labyrinth of forgotten memories. His revelations shed light on the rich African culture that existed prior to the painful era of slavery. *Roots* offered hope to a multitude of disillusioned people of the African Diaspora.

As with any new revelation, the historical accuracy of *Roots* was not without controversy. His book was affirming, so I put aside the negative rhetoric, and became a firm believer in what Alex Haley had accomplished. I, too, would try to trace my roots from America to the West Indies and, hopefully, back to Africa.

West Africans were primarily oral historians, and events pertaining to their history and familial lineage were passed on by spoken word. The *griot* served as the musician, the teller of stories, and the historian. Torn from their homes and enslaved in a system of bondage that was often cruel and sadistic, the Africans were forbidden to openly practice their traditions. To maintain control, their captors exploited the African slaves and led them to believe they were less than nothing. The family unit was unraveled, and their connections to their religion, language, music, food, became fleeting memories. The stories, if they were to be told, would now be predicated on acts of violence, poverty, rape, and illegitimacy.

'My roots I'll never forget.
I'll always remember the road I traveled.'
— Burning Spear

The sudden and overwhelming loss of self-respect resulted in creating a race of people who became silent about the past. Stories and secrets that elicited feelings of shame and guilt often died with the ancestors. Yet, despite this dilemma, in most families of the African Diaspora, stories have survived.

Growing up, I heard bits and pieces of stories about ancestors. The game "Telephone," where a message is whispered from one player to the next, with the final player announcing the message he or she heard, is an example of how much an original message can change. Distortions and embellishments are the most compelling difficulties that can arise when depending solely on oral histories.

When I began doing genealogy research, I decided that, rather than discount family oral accounts, I would try to find as much corroborating documentation as I could.

"Baba," a Barbados slave, was said to have been the unofficial ruler on one of the Prout properties, either "Mess House" in St. George's parish, or "Arise & Trade," in the parish of St. Thomas. The tale extolled Baba, who, after being sold, refused to get out of the cart when she arrived at the house of her new Prout owner. It appears that Baba had previously worked on a much larger estate and found her new abode less than suitable.

The tale of a black slave woman, who, despite her low status, had the nerve to express her dissatisfaction was a story worth repeating. It has been told and retold for well over a century and a half. Given the horrors of the institution of slavery, the story of Baba was uplifting. She was rebellious, outspoken, and, although held in bondage, held herself in high esteem.

Whether the legendary Baba was a myth or a reality became a burning question that I wanted to try to answer.

BARBARDOS, BRITISH WEST INDIES, was the birthplace of my maternal grandmother, Edith Nurse Prout, and she always referred to it as "home." She was the *griot* of our family, the keeper of the memories, the story teller. Barbados was still a British colony, and my childhood memories of my first visit are of learning the monetary system—tuppence, fivepence, and shillings—and of the warm turquoise blue ocean. Most of all, I remember meeting many of the relations I had heard my grandmother talk about.

Many years later, when I decided to trace my roots, the first person I talked to was my Barbados maternal grandmother. Although she kept insisting that my many questions were taxing her brain, she provided me with enough information to begin my search. My next step was to get a clear understanding of the island's history and culture, particularly relating to the slave era and the time that Baba would have lived (abt. 1790s-1880s). Without this historical information, it would be difficult to put Baba's life into context.

Barbados is a small coral island divided into eleven parishes that encompasses an area of fourteen-by-twenty-one square miles, and it has the distinction of having no claim by Christopher Columbus of discovery. The original inhabitants had been the Arawaks.

By 1627, however, when the first European and African settlers arrived—comprising eighty British subjects and ten African prize slaves who had been captured en route to the island—Barbados was uninhabited.

The rapid growth of the sugar cane industry necessitated the importation of more Africans, who proved to be better suited to toil in the blazing sun than were the fair-skinned European indentured servants.

The laws pertaining to the slave trade and slavery were somewhat complicated. In 1807, for example, the slave trade in the British Caribbean was abolished, but slavery was not. Simplified, it meant that if you already owned slaves, you could legally keep them, but you were not allowed to import new slaves. This law was difficult to enforce, and illegal slave trading continued. As a solution to the problem, in 1814, the British government required that anyone who owned slaves had to register their number. The registration included their names, gender, color, age, occupation, and place of birth.

By 1816, slavery still existed in the British Caribbean, but there was growing controvery about the moral, social, and ethical implications of enslaving human beings. That same year, the slaves, tired of being exploited, became more rebellious, and masterminded a number of violent uprisings on the island.

It wasn't until 1817 that all slave owners in the British Caribbean complied with the law and submitted their Slave Registers to the British Crown. These lists were to be updated every three years, and the slave owners were to explain any increase or decrease in the original number of slaves they registered.

The next important historical event was that slavery was abolished in 1833; this took effect in 1834. Prior to the abolition of slavery, a slave owner could *manumit* (legally free) a slave. In some cases, slaves purchased their own freedom

I found it ironic that the former slaves were not granted complete freedom. From 1834 until 1838, there was what was termed "a transition period," where they continued to work as apprentices for their former masters. The former slaves were paid a small wage and given other minor benefits. Because there were many problems with trying to maintain control under apprenticeship, they were granted full freedom in 1838.

In 1990, I made my first visit to the Barbados Archives, in Black Rock (formerly St. Michael and now rezoned), St. James. Prior to being housed in the archives, all records—the parochial registers of baptisms, marriages, and burials—were kept in the various parish churches, with the Church of England (Anglican) being the official religious denomination during the era of slavery.

Because the institution of slavery was such a profitable business, meticulous financial records were maintained by the slave owners to be sent to Great Britain. The majority of these records pertaining to slavery and the slave trade are housed at the Public Record Office (PRO), now the National Archives, in England.

The only surviving census document that I found was the one from 1715, and it only lists the white inhabitants, so I had to depend on other records to validate events and familial connections. Armed with this information, I was ready to do battle, and begin my search for Baba.

Documents Used to Find Baba

I began my research using slave baptism records and located a Prout slave owner. "On 24th June, 1832, in the parish of St. Thomas, Barbados ____ Prout[1] (no given name was documented) baptizes five coloured children, Eliza, George, James, Frances, Sarah, and one negro child, Melinda, as his slaves."

At the PRO, I located records that conclusively identified Joseph Benjamin Prout as the slave owner. In his 1817 Slave Register[2], he reported having five slaves; among them is a slave named "Barbara," who I surmised could be the infamous Baba: "Barbara, Female, Black, Domestic, thirty years, Barbadian." Also listed are "Peggy Ann, Female, Black, Field, twenty-six years, Barbadian; Benny, Male, Black, Domestic, four years, Barbadian; Jacob, Male, Black, Domestic, one year, Barbadian; and Rachael, Female, Black, Domestic, one year, Barbadian."

Consulting the Deed Books at the Barbados Archives, I found

103

records that indicated that in 1814, on the fifth day of May, BENJAMIN JOSEPH PROUT purchased a slave, BARBARA, from JOHN YEARWOOD SEARLES for eighty-five Pounds.[3]

Backtracking, I located a sale in 1810, the sixth day of October, of a Negro woman slave, BARBARA, by SAMUEL DRAYTON to JOHN YEARWOOD SEARLES for one-hundred Pounds.[4]

In this case, I speculate that a reason SEARLES, after paying one-hundred Pounds for BARBARA, might have sold her four years later to BENJAMIN JOSEPH PROUT for eight-five Pounds was that BARBARA was the type of person who might refuse to get out of a cart.

On the 1834 Slave Return of JOSEPH "PROUTE," he lists twenty-three slaves. BARBARA, age forty-seven, and RACHEL, age eighteen, are among them. An 1840[6] record of baptism indicates that RACHEL (an adult) was baptised and is the daughter of BARBARA. In 1842, RACHEL dies, and on her burial record[7], she is identified as RACHAEL PROUT.

The 1864 will of JOSEPH BENJAMIN PROUT[8] doesn't mention BARBARA. He bequeaths his estate to twelve "reputed children." Among them are two daughters named SARAH and a son named GEORGE. In his 1834 Slave Return,[9] I see listed GEORGE as 3 $6/12$ coloured, and SARAH as 3 $6/12$ coloured.

Another door has opened: Was JOSEPH BENJAMIN PROUT the father of the slaves GEORGE and SARAH?

We, the people of the African Diaspora, must not lose sight of our rich oral tradition. We must set the tone and preserve our family histories honestly and respectfully. We must keep in mind that the same establishment that said we had no history, decided in the 1930s to validate segments of our history. Our ancestors' stories were documented in the form of the "Slave Narrative." We must assume the role and responsibilities of the *griot* by continuing to tell the stories—and also committing them to paper.

REFERENCES

1. Baptisms/Marriages/Burials, St. Thomas, Barbados, 1728-1852, *LDS File: 1157946 Nos. 1371-1376, pp. 505-6.*

2. Slave Return 1817, Public Record Office (PRO), Kew, England, T71/522/94.

3. Deed 1814, Barbados Archives, Black Rock, St. James, Barbados W.I., RB1/255/259.

4. Deed 1810, Barbados Archives, Black Rock, St. James, Barbados. W.I. RB1/287/95.

5. Slave Return 1834, PRO, Kew, England, T72/557/9.

6. Baptisms/Marriages/Burials, St. Thomas, Barbados, 1728-1852. *p. 261, LDS File: 1157946.*

7. Burial 1842, St. George, Barbados, Barbados Archives, Black Rock, St. James, Barbados, W.I. RL1/56/331.

8 Will 1864, Barbados Archives, Black Rock, St. James, Barbados, RB4/78. p. 553.

9. Slave Return 1834, PRO, Kew, England, T711/557/9.

Humor

Write a wise saying,
and your name will live forever.
— Anonymous

HERE I COME, READY OR NOT

by Shelley Simon
Seattle, Washington
2004

I emerged from a better place on October 3rd, 1940. If my mother were still here, she could describe it to you, my emergence, not the better place. I remember none of it. She said the doctor handed me to her, and first thing she noticed, I was a snot-nosed kid. Forty-three years later, I'd have surgery to open my right nostril, the one that ran when I didn't. Until then, I couldn't chug-a-lug beer, but that was the only benefit.

My parents named me Ira Shelley. My first name displeased my father's powerful sister Nora, who decided my first name should be Shelley, and so it became. Despite having seen my birth certificate many times, I thought Shelley was my first name. When I was sixty I noticed my first name was actually Ira. I'm happy about the switch because people don't confuse me with retirement funds or the Irish Republican Army.

Does anyone remember much about the earliest years of life?

The "preverts" among us would want to remember breast-feeding, but let's concentrate on we who are normal, or so we think. The first ten years of my life, we lived on a block from which families rarely moved. My parents, two brothers, and I occupied the second floor apartment of a two-flat on Central Park Avenue in Chicago's Albany Park. Nate was two-and-one-half-years older than I and occasionally we played together, but had friends in common only when we were young children. Ted was five years older than I and read constantly. Late at night, he'd read in bed under the covers with a flashlight or he'd sit in the hallway, reading under a dim blue ceiling light, trying to satisfy an early, healthy curiosity. The landlord provided little heat at night, and on wintry mornings, my brothers and I dressed beneath the covers. Heaven would have been underwear preheated by a heating pad.

In the living room were built-in bookcases on each side of the fireplace. The "logs" were made of cement and didn't burn well. The kitchen stove was pastel green, with burners on the right side and oven on the left at eye level. I don't know if the gas oven was that high to make it easier to cook in, or easier to stick your head in. There were three bedrooms, one occupied by my parents, one by Ted, and one shared by Nate and me. Over my parents' bed hung a large print of a tall slender woman in wide-brimmed, white hat, and pink gown, lounging on a loveseat with two white greyhounds at her feet. Where do you find such a person? There was little room in the bedroom Nate and I shared, and from the ceiling hung stick model airplanes we'd built. When we tired of a plane, we took it to a high place, set it on fire, and threw it, a fighter flaming down in a World War II movie.

Friends and I often played in the alley where we could hear our mothers' calls. Weekly, the junkman came down the alley, with a wagon pulled by an enormous draft horse. His hooves with their light-colored hair resembled bell-bottoms, and I loved their clomping on the pavement. I was entranced by the sounds from his mouth, sounds no language can duplicate or describe. In winter, twin plumes of steam shot from his nostrils. He had leather straps running every which way across his body. He would have been attractive to a female horse into kinky sex. I didn't like all that on him. The man yelled, "Any old clothes to sell?" He also sharpened knives and scissors on a grinding wheel. I hoped his horse would escape someday.

Sometimes coal would be delivered in the alley, in a pile at the entrance to someone's yard. A man with a shovel and wheelbarrow was left to move the coal into the buyer's coal shed. It would take him hours and on hot days, his skin would be damp and coal dust dark. I hoped he'd escape someday, too.

My kindergarten teacher at Haugan School was Mrs. Kelly, a tall, slender, soft-spoken woman of beginning-to-gray hair, who was always kind to the children. She brought her piano to the class to teach music. When I visited the school in 1983, I found that her piano was still at the school. Despite her age (early nineties), she met regularly with the school's teachers and was active in school affairs. Oh, to be in kindergarten again, listening to Mrs. Kelly beating the tom-tom as my class marches about the room, and knowing my mittens are securely attached to the ends of my coat sleeves.

There were five movie theaters nearby: the Terminal, the Metro, the Alba, the Admiral, and the Drake. The lowest admission price I recall was eleven cents, for a double feature and a serial. The Terminal and Metro were across the street from one another. The Terminal was a large theater with grand balcony, staircase, and lobby of Renaissance-revival ornateness. The Metro, a smaller theater, was unusual because the screen was on the same wall as the entry doors into the seating area. My brother Ted claims when I was five, I embarrassed him by asking the usher, "Usher, where's the duty room?" The Alba on Kedzie Avenue was converted into a bowling alley. The Terminal, Metro, and Drake were converted to shops over the years. Only the Admiral perseveres, now showing porno films—the only theater remaining in the neighborhood, saved by depravity.

Lawrence Avenue was the equivalent of today's mall. It differed in that you walked rather than driving, you brought a shopping cart rather than your drug of choice, you met people you knew, the store owners called you by name, you got wet when it rained, and it smelled of food not chemicals. Becker's Bakery sold a cinnamon loaf that I'd consider committing foul play to obtain. Louie's Produce Market had it all and it was all naturally raised. No one had figured out how to raise unnatural produce yet. At the kosher butcher shop the chickens were alive (Do kids today know that chickens used to have feet?) and my mother would choose a chicken after going eye to eye with it. The butcher would painlessly (It was painless to me. I'm not certain if the chicken thought so.) behead the chicken and sometimes the chicken would run a bit before realizing things weren't the same. A tall, slender, gray-haired man working for the butcher delivered meat on his bicycle, which had a huge basket on the front. He wore a dirty, long, white butcher's coat and his name was Chicken Tony. I wonder if his mother named him that.

One endless summer day in Chicago when I was four, I was playing hide-and-go-seek with friends from the block. I looked up and saw my mother step out onto the back stairs. Her eyes were filled with tears and she called out that President Roosevelt had died! It was the first time I'd seen my mother cry and it would forever place the presidency on a par with angels. Since Roosevelt, lesser men have held the office, but to me it will always be holy, baptized by my mother's tears.

When I was six, one chilly spring day I entered our basement with Nate and heard faint sounds, *meooow, meooow*. We followed the sounds to two tiny, hairless, pink kittens, eyes closed, lying on a pile of rags. They were the offspring of a stray cat in our neighborhood. We went into the yard and saw Mike the janitor coming down the alley.

Nate said, "Mike, there's kittens in the basement and we don't know what to do with them."

He said, "Show me," and followed us into the basement. Without a word, he threw open the furnace door and shoveled the kittens into the flames. If Nate and I had done nothing, the kittens would have been alive! What kind of man would do such a thing in front of two small children? If I hadn't seen it, I wouldn't believe that such a monster could exist!!

I used to go to my maternal grandmother's home by myself. I don't know how old she was, but to a six-year-old she looked ancient. Of average height and somewhat overweight, she walked with a slight limp and, to my knowledge, never left the apartment she shared with my mother's brother and sister. She wore slightly worn, but clean, floral-patterned house dresses, and her hair was gray here and white there with no apparent plan. She was always pleased by my enormous appetite for her cooking. Unkind words never emerged from her lips; the enchanted grandmother-grand-child filter sanctified everything she said.

We would play five-hundred-rummy and she'd feed me the absolute greatest chicken soup there ever could be. The Mona Lisa of chicken soup. Don't tell me your grandmother's chicken soup was better. You're nuts. While eating, I glanced at the wall calendar showing a Russell painting, the one of the cowpoke on horseback, looking over the Grand Canyon. I knew I'd go there some day.

My other grandparents had died before I was born. In 1950, when I was nine, my grandmother died, but I never learned the cause. My parents, being protective, said I didn't have to attend the funeral and I don't remember if I did or not. I was sad, but not devastated, because I had family near. I was confused because I wasn't sure how to behave around my mother. Was there something I was supposed to do for her?

In summer when I was eight, Ted decided to build a soapbox car, and Nate and I could help. Ted drew plans, getting assistance from his six-million books, and became the foreman keeping watch on his slaves. We used only hand saws. Though children, we didn't need power tools like the pansy carpenters do today. It could seat two riders and had no brakes, but kids never stop anyway. On a near-by hill we took turns and suffered no casualties. I'd give a million for that car today. I don't know what happened to it, probably cannibal-ized for some torture apparatus for the dungeon.

In those early years, my positive experiences outweighed the negative ones. I'd seen some horrors at a very young age, but wasn't badly scarred. Unfortunately, the type of projects I was involved in aren't always available to children whose three-dimensional lives are often replaced by two-dimensional screens. I don't think a computer screen is much better for a child than a TV screen, neither being reality.

But then how would I know? I'm not a kid anymore.

AUNT MABEL'S OUTHOUSE

by Norma Ann Van Wilgen Hanson
Clarks Grove, Minnesota
2002

My family lived in Minnesota and Aunt Mabel lived on an Iowa farm. Aunt Mabel was quite the woman. She cooked, cleaned, gardened, raised a family, kept animals of all kinds, farmed, trapped and hunted, was an active member of her church, a helpful neighbor, and was always a gracious hostess to guests.

We always looked forward to our trips to Aunt Mabel's Iowa farm several times during the year, to celebrate a birthday or a gathering of the relatives for a picnic reunion or just to visit and share good home cooking.

Our trips to the Iowa farm meant I could visit Aunt Mabel's fancy outhouse. It was my favorite thing on that Iowa farm. If only my playhouse at home were as nice as that outhouse. Aunt Mabel did not call it "The Outhouse." That name didn't sound ladylike to my aunt. It was called The Biffy, or Mrs. Murphy, and it was Aunt Mabel's pride and joy.

This outhouse was not your ordinary, run-of-the-mill outhouse by any means. This outhouse, mind you, was a thing to behold. It was built on a foundation, with wooden siding and a shingled roof. It had two small windows, located high up, of course, not the tacky half-moon cut into the door like some outhouses. Some had no windows at all to let in the light, except maybe cracks in the walls where the light filtered in, and at night, complete darkness. Other outhouses had cracks in their walls that let in the winter snow and howling wind, but not this outhouse.

When electricity came to the farm, of course the outhouse was wired and had a single light bulb, turned on with a long, hanging string, for visits in the dark. A brick path led the way from the back door of the house to the outhouse, and it seemed a long way to me as a little girl.

In the spring and summer, pots of flowers sat on the outhouse steps as a cheerful and colorful welcome. Aunt Mabel made curtains for the outhouse windows out of flowered feed sacks, selected at the local feed store. The curtains were always clean, freshly starched, and ironed. The walls were wallpapered in flowers, of course— would it be anything else? The wallpaper and curtains matched the flowers that Mabel planted in every available spot, and around every building on the farm.

Flies? Not in this outhouse. A sticky spiraled flypaper hung in a corner to catch any intruder flies that may have entered the outhouse. The only sound was the soft hum of those flies stuck to the flypaper. There were no spiders or their telltale webs in Aunt Mabel's outhouse, as were found in everyone else's. She kept the outhouse spotless, scrubbing it weekly.

As everyone did at that time, Aunt Mabel saved her outdated Montgomery Ward and Sears catalogs, the pages being the toilet paper, first reading and then wiping. I think maybe the young boys would have eyed the women's underwear pages, the men the latest in farm equipment, and the women the latest in washing machines and house dresses. Even more special and appreciated were the soft tissue-like peach papers, instead of the scratchy catalog pages. In the late summer, peaches were bought in a box, each peach wrapped separately. The peaches were canned and the precious peach papers saved for the outhouse. What a treat—the peaches and the paper. Store-bought toilet paper was brought to the outhouse when special company or the "Ladies Aid" came to visit.

But the best part were the holes. This outhouse was a "three holer"! One hole built low for children, the middle hole regular height and the third hole was built higher for the tall people. All were arranged in a stair step fashion and painted a soft grey. All three had round lids made of wood to cover the holes. Of course, the holes were cut small, medium and large, so the little ones would not fall in. I tried the highest one. Didn't everybody?

The outhouse was built on a foundation, and was a permanent building, unlike the outhouses we and all our neighbors, friends, and relatives had. Outhouses were built to be moved when the hole got almost full. A new hole was dug and the old hole topped off with dirt. (I wonder if that spot was marked somehow so unsuspecting people didn't plunge into the guck.) The outhouse was then moved onto a newly dug hole for a new beginning.

Aunt Mabel's outhouse seems to have always been there, a symbol of farm living. Eventually, much-appreciated modern plumbing came to the house, but the old outhouse still stood, neat, clean, painted, and with flowers encircling it. The farm is now rented out and there was talk of tearing down the old outhouse, but the family decided it must stay, and it still stands today as a monument to Aunt Mabel!

Aunt Mabel lived on that Iowa farm until she became ill and went to a nursing home. She died there still talking about the farm, her animals, her gardens, and her outhouse—and how much she missed everything and wanted to go back some day.

ONE BITE

by John Sheirer,
Enfield, Connecticut
2004

Back in my college days, partly on a dare, partly from fatigue, and partly for love, I ate an entire jelly donut in one bite. Three friends and I had gone to an all-night donut shop to blow off steam during final exams week. I guess we weren't terribly rebellious, considering there were about a dozen bars in the area. But who needs alcohol when there are donuts to be consumed?

We were the only customers in the place at two-thirty a.m., each of us munching on about our fourth donut. The combination of study fatigue, suddenly full stomachs, and post-sugar buzz had set in hard, so we were in danger of falling asleep right there at our table. Something had to be done to liven us up before we drove back to the dorm to continue studying.

I slammed both palms on the stained Formica and announced, "I can eat an entire jelly donut in one bite!"

My friends jumped about six inches out of their seats, swore at me, and then started protesting.

"No one can do that!" Sarah cried.

"I say pooh-pooh on your donut!" Mike ranted. (I am translating Mike's more colorful comment into family-history-friendly language.) Mike was pre-med. He had taken a biology final the previous day and a chemistry final that morning, and he was dreading a physics final the following afternoon. His head was stuffed with science, and he moved between anger and frustration, shouts and tears, more than a few times that week.

"If you can do it," Susan said with a smile, "I just might marry you."

"Why?" Sarah asked.

"Think about it," Susan replied.

"Oh," Sarah said.

Mike tried for a few seconds, but his brain didn't have room to work out what they meant. I had only a slight inkling, but that inkling certainly made me look at Susan in a new way.

Sarah pushed a blueberry-filled pastry toward me. Blueberry was my favorite. It was the last one left on the table.

"I've been saving this one," she said. "If you can eat it in one bite, I won't marry you, but I'll give you a dollar."

"Me too!" Mike and Sarah chimed. Three dollars—this was getting interesting. I was a poor college student who saw actual paper money about twice a month. Three whole dollars qualified as an academic scholarship.

The donut was about four inches in diameter and two inches thick. Powdered sugar covered the surface, and blueberry jelly oozed from a dime-sized navel on one side. The thing looked pretty darned big as I examined it. Under normal circumstances, I would have needed maybe seven or eight good bites to get it down. But then I'd probably think, "Wow, that was so small. How about another?"

I picked it up. It seemed to weigh a pound because, I guess, jelly is heavy stuff. Three pairs of measuring eyes darted back and forth from my mouth to the donut. I turned the navel toward me to prevent spillage and brought it to my lips.

On the first push, a third of the donut easily entered my mouth, but then I encountered resistance. I had to shove first the left side and then the right side to keep it advancing beyond the corners of my mouth.

This trundle method worked fine until the donut encountered my epiglottis, the little flap of flesh at the back of the throat. I began to gag. It took all my self-control to keep from yanking the thing out of my mouth. At this point, the first tear plopped out of my eye and flowed down my cheek.

I kept pushing.

The donut crammed up against the back of my throat and started expanding upward into my pallet and downward into and under my tongue. By then, it had lost most of its structural integrity, becoming nothing more than a fused blob of pastry and jelly conforming to the inside of my mouth.

The tears began to flow freely now, and some sort of liquid threatened to spill from my nose as well. I sniffled as forcefully as I could, snorting up a big dose of powdered sugar in the process. Every force in my body urged me to get the thing out of my mouth.

But I kept pushing.

A few more tucks at each corner, and the donut was inside. I clasped my teeth together and sealed my lips.

"Oh, Lord," Mike gasped.

"He did it," Sarah said.

"Not yet," Susan cut in. "I won't marry him unless he swallows."

The three of them began chanting, *"swallow, swallow, swallow."* They began in a whisper, then built to a low moan. *"Swallow, swallow, swallow."*

For human beings, chewing usually precedes swallowing. I parted my teeth and closed them again, then repeated the movement a few times, being careful not to open my lips—not out of politeness, but to keep donut paste from spraying across the room.

Normally, the tongue is used to roll the food around the mouth so that it gets ground up by the teeth. But this takes lots of open space, something I had none of in my mouth, filled as it was with donut. My chewing efforts managed only to mush up the small fraction of pastry directly between my molars.

In short, the whole mess was stuck in my mouth with no real way for me to chew it. In fact, it was actually expanding as it soaked up my saliva at an alarming rate. To keep my cheeks from bursting open, I had to do something fast.

"*Swallow, swallow, swallow,*" they chanted.

My gag reflex came to my rescue. As I involuntarily tightened the back of my throat, I could feel those muscles smashing a small portion of the donut back there. In desperation, I clamped down harder and found I could actually "chew" with my throat muscles.

After a few more contractions, the donut was soft enough to get some down. I swallowed a small portion, freeing up enough mouth space to guide more donut to the back of my throat where I muscle-chewed and swallowed a bit more.

"*Swallow, swallow, swallow.*"

I then discovered that I had just barely enough room to do a little traditional teeth chewing. This was tough going, but it began to work. Bit by bit, I managed to swallow more and more of the donut until the task didn't seem quite so impossible.

"Oh my Lord," Sarah muttered, breaking the chant. "I think he's going to do it."

It took another full minute, but I was able to get the rest of the thing swallowed. My throat burned. My face was streaked with tears. Sometime during the process, I had lost control of my nose. The results were not pretty.

Susan grabbed a handful of napkins and mopped my face. "That was amazing!" she said, leaning in to kiss me on the cheek. When she pulled away, I saw tiny flecks of powdered sugar on her lips. I'd never really looked at Susan's lips before, but I was having trouble looking anywhere else at that moment. Her tongue slipped out to lick the sugar from her lower lip, the fuller of the two.

"I don't believe it," Mike said. "Make him open his mouth."

Susan gently grasped my jaw, and I opened my mouth to display its lack of donut.

"Ugh," Sarah moaned. Apparently, there was still some donut

residue in there. I took a swig of hot chocolate (now cold), rinsed it around my mouth, swallowed, and opened again.

"I wouldn't have believed it," Mike murmured.

"He did it!" Sarah cried.

The three of them broke into applause, nearly awakening the high school kid snoozing through his late-night shift behind the counter.

Susan gathered up the three one-dollar bills from the table and tucked them into her shirt pocket.

"I'll just hold onto these," she said. "My abnormal psych final is over at noon tomorrow. If you meet me at the student union, I'll buy you an ice cream cone." She winked at me. "I'm dying to see what you can do with that."

NAMES OF YORE

by Marlene Brooks Brannon
Oceanside, California
2003

There's nothing like a baby on the way to get folks' knickers in a knot about names. When my daughter Amy was expecting, she and her husband, Bryan, were obsessed with perusing names in baby books. I, however—being one of you and therefore of unsound mind—went straight to the genealogy files. What I found, dear hearts, is that we just don't see names anymore like those names of yore. I love that word *yore*, although in my native South, it doesn't mean "long ago" as defined by Webster's Collegiate. What it means is "not belonging to me," as in, "Is this yore hat? It ain't mine." But I digress.

I found some marvelous names in those dusty files. Lovely old names like Temperance and Valusia and Celestra, and three sisters named Lumina Emma, Ollie Pearl, and Clara Bell. I found Chloe Adeline and Chloe Cornelia, Lucretia Cornelia and Massena Cordelia. I found peculiar names like Narcissa Heneretta and Louisa Arcajah and Belzia Jane. And I found some downright ugly names, too, like Mahulda Luazy and Thurza. Lordy, lordy. Why would a loving parent foist those names on a newborn babe?

I found a Hattie Beulah, a Beulah Viola, and my favorites: Eula Livonia, Eula Grace, and Lily Grace. If I had heard those names before my daughters were born, I would have surely named one of them Lily Grace. Now my only hope for a Lily Grace is to get a cat. And, before I forget—oh my goodness—Sophronia and Salemanthia, Asenath, and Meridith Ithamar. Can you imagine more lyrical names than Sophronia and Salemanthia or Asenath and Meridith Ithamar? I love the thound of thoth nameth ath they roll off oneth tongue and juth thort of hang thuthpended in the air like muthical noteth.

Joel and Henrietta Kay blessed most of their children with reasonably agreeable names—Robert, Mary, William, Ann, and Emma—nothing unusual. But somewhere along the way, one of them must have had a heat stroke. They named one of their daughters Urania. Now I don't know about you, but to me Urania approaches the boundaries of decency. On the other side of the coin, Charles Abner Kay named his children Luther, Ernest, Silas, Mamie, and Nannie. Then he had a temporary period of sanity and named his last child James.

I found some men's names that are real lulus. I found Jeremiah and Hezekiah and Amaziah and Elias. I found Eustis and Clement Thoeophilus and Percival and Enoch and Wister and Silas Erasmus and Nimrod. I don't know if it's a perverted mind, a twisted sense of humor, or onset of dementia that would cause a couple to saddle their spawn with Silas Erasmus. And who in their right mind would name a little boy Nimrod? Rather than a name for a child, it sounds more like something you would say to a child. Example: "How many times have I told you to put that hammer back where you found it, you nimrod."

My friend and fellow scribe Sandra Carpenter once opened a story about her grandmother Effie with this line: *Death was Grandma's hobby.* What a great line and what a great name! You just know that Effie was a woman who meant business. Although they didn't know each other, Effie shared a hobby with my late funeral-fanatic, tomb-tending aunt Billie Brooks. Comforting the aggrieved was a lifelong passion for Effie and Billie. These two wake-watchers allowed no death to go unheralded, no dearly departed unmourned, nor any mourner unfed.

My grandmother, Mama Hattie—and we'll get to her name in just a minute—used to tell the grandchildren a story about a girl whose mother was so intimidated by the squabbling aunts, she named her daughter after all of them. The child was named Careful-Julie-Ginny-Lizzie-Roxy-Ann-Missouri. Talk about a muddled moniker. This girl's mother needed therapy. Assertiveness training comes to mind.

Mama Hattie's name was Harriett Ava Matilda Landrum Brooks. She so wanted one of the grandchildren named after her (and none of her children obliged her) that by the time I came along, she was offering money. I'm guessing the stakes weren't high enough.

Mama and Daddy were for the most part traditional name-givers, naming us Charlotte Ann, John Gordon, and Marlene. They did go a little off center with my older brother's name, which is Maxie. Not Maximillian. Not Maxwell. Just Maxie. I thought it was Mama's doing, but she told me that it was actually my dad's idea. Daddy was a boxing fan and Maxie was named after a prizefighter my dad admired.

For some reason, I—unlike my brothers and my sister—was not given a middle name. I felt a little deprived. I remember asking my dad what my middle name was and he said "Narion." Although the choice was a bit odd, I was happy to find out I did have a middle name. I was also ticked off to find out that my mother—who insisted I did not have a middle name—was a liar. It turned out that Mama wasn't a liar. Daddy was. And a tease. What he said was *nary 'un.*

There are certain girls' names that have been in style throughout the years. In my research for a baby name, I found a lot of Sarahs and Elizabeths and Emmas. In more recent years, we've had the Stacy-Tracy-Stephanie decade, which slid into the Jennifer-Heather era. That gave way to the Michelle-Nicole-Amy period. Now we seem to be riding out the Tiffany-Brandy years.

I'll admit I succumbed to the trends, naming my daughters Stephanie and Amy. Amy's grandmothers' names are Alma Lou and Mattie Lou. That made it easy to kiss up to both grannies by naming my daughter Amy Lou. No money was forthcoming.

My Stephanie's son's name is Jeffrey Ernest Borgnine. The name "Ernest" is a tad out of vogue in my view, but he was named after his paternal grandpa of *Marty* and *McHale's Navy* fame. Jeff—aged ten—is beginning to realize that his name will get him a certain amount of attention, but Jeff doesn't know *Marty* from Smarty and I doubt if he's even seen *McHale's Navy*. What impresses Jeff is that his Pa Ernie is the voice of Mermaid Man on *SpongeBob SquarePants*.

Well, the long and short of it is that Amy and Bryan didn't appreciate my offerings from the genealogy files. They went with a good Irish name—Aiden—for their little boy. I didn't get my britches in a bunch. I'm just glad they didn't sabotage my grandson by hanging him with a handle like Silas Erasmus. Or Nimrod.

PS: If I've used yore name, I hope you ain't offended.

RESOURCES

The "vintage" names of yore came from <u>Descendants of Robert Kay of South Carolina</u>, 2nd Ed., 1999, James E. Kay, William D. Kay, Jeremiah A. Kay, Franklin A. Spearman, Carl B. Kay.

Teaching on Guam

by Kenneth F. Harris
Tuscon, Arizona
2003

My wife and I taught for four years on the island of Guam, from 1970 to 1974. Our children attended the local public schools. My wife taught at one of the two island high schools. I taught elementary school, and, since I was the union shop steward, when the chance came to put me in an "annex" in the jungle two miles from the main school, the administration fell on the opportunity with gusto.

I am writing the memoirs of this and other experiences for my granddaughters to read and enjoy in some distant time and place.

DID I MENTION THAT WE HAD JOBS on Guam as teachers? That's what we went out there for, not the travel, the scuba diving, the parties, or the fun. But all teachers were not in agreement about the goal. I felt that I was out to give the best lessons I possibly could according to the adopted (and frequently adapted) Department of Education curriculum. It was not my job to teach the kids the values and ethics of white, middle-class Milwaukee. I mention Milwaukee because I had a discussion with a first-grade teacher who felt precisely the opposite. She felt it was her goal, her duty, her mission, to teach the children to "do like they do in Milwaukee."

We certainly had the materials to do exactly that. All of our texts were Mainland published and Mainland specific. I presented two pictures to my second graders, one of a forest and one of a subsequent clear cut. I asked them which came first, and they had no idea. They lived on an island where jungle vegetation was cleared or burned deliberately and reappeared within a couple of seasons. Our book told them about cows in the dairy. The class jumped up and down and swore there were no cows in the dairy. They had been to the dairy on a field trip the year before, and there were no cows at the dairy! They were quite correct, of course. The dairy on Guam is a reconstituting plant. Milk is received in powdered form, mixed with water, and sent out to the stores. What a stupid book.

And there were some real cultural differences as well. A friend of mine taught ESL (English as a Second Language) at Ordot-Chalan Pago School using SRA material. SRA (I forget what the letters stand for) material is very structured and presents a basic English program that would be totally approved of in Milwaukee. The teacher holds up a card toward the class. In front of the card is a picture for the class to see; in back of the card is a question for the teacher to ask and an answer to receive. The teacher is required to ask the question exactly as written, and to accept no other answer except the one on the card, exactly as written. ESL classes are filled with people who speak another language at home and who are not succeeding in the mainstream program.

So here's what happened to my friend. He held up a card with a picture of a dog. He read the question, shrugged, and asked, "Is this food?" The question resulted in one of the best classroom discussions he had all year. There were some Chamorros, some Filipinos, some Palauans, and they all had different views. In general, Chamorros couldn't see eating a dog when there was an abundance of chickens around. Some of the Filipinos throught it was a pretty

126

skinny dog, and the Palauans thought it depended on how you fixed them.

Then there was an ear difference. I heard sounds differently from my class. Most of them couldn't tell "once" from "wants." The words were homophones as far as the class was concerned, which made teaching spelling a bit of a challenge. And I remember one February talking about Lincoln and how his attitude was set for life when he saw a slave market. I went on and on for five minutes about Lincoln and the slave market. The kids looked blank. Polite, but blank. I finally asked them what they thought a slave was. Silence. Finally, one little boy ventured an opinion. "What Santa drives?" Well, there's another lesson shot in the tail because I didn't check student understanding before I began.

The difference in hearing sounds between Mainlanders and Islanders led to some quaint expressions. One of my favorites was *"boo shed."* an expletive denoting the alimentary extrusions of a male bovie. Then there's, "let's give him the clap," for "let's give him a hand." "Birds of a feather get stuck together" was another personal favorite. "Yes, me," was another phrase I liked. It meant, "I also agree with your dubious proposal," or, "Well, if we're all having thirds on the ice cream, I supposed I might as well."

English spoken this way can be remarkably effective. I remember a second-grade girl running up to me on the playground, pulling out my shirt, and commenting, "Eee, Mr. Harris, plenty belly." Then she ran around behind me and pulled out my shirt. "Plenty belly back here, too." I've thought and thought, but I don't see how she could have expressed herself more effectively.

The teacher next door to me was and is one of my all-time favorite human beings. I've tried writing this without using her name, but it just doesn't work. Mrs. Shackelford taught the "slow" third grade. She was an immense woman, and every ounce was filled with good humor and love for her students and mankind in general. In short, she was exactly the kind of person you don't want to make angry. People who are angry all the time know very well what they're doing and how to do it. But Mrs. Shackelford only got angry

127

once in her life, so I have heard. And she didn't do it very well. She overreacted. Probably lack of practice.

Here's the story I heard. I wasn't there, thanks be. Apparently a ruling came down from on high that Chamorros who married Mainlanders lost their citizenship. This matter of citizenship on Guam or the U.S.A. came up every now and again. It was a curious situation, and I just don't have the time to write three books about it. In this case, the ruling impacted Mrs. Shackelford's rights to attend the University of Guam to gain a teaching credential. But mostly, the ruling affected her pride. She was a Chamorro lady, and nobody was going to take that away from her. I understand that she decided to pay a call on the attorney general. She didn't make an appointment. And she didn't bother the secretary when she got there; she announced herself. She expressed herself vigorously and in just a very few minutes, the attorney general discovered he had an appointment elsewhere. As he left, he directed his secretary to find out what that woman wanted and give it to her.

Sometimes it pays to vent your anger. But most of the time, Mrs. Shackelford and anger were not even speaking acquaintances. I remember once the smallest boy in her third grade ran to her crying, brushing dirt off his body, complaining that the biggest boy in the class, Gregory, had pushed him down. Mrs. S. did not ground Gregory forever and then hug and mother the little boy, as I expected. Instead, she hugged the big boy. She said, "Gregory, you go over there and hug that little boy and say, "I'm sorry, boy, I won't hurt you any more." And Gregory did exactly that. And he lived up to his word, too. The little boy was safe from Gregory's untender ministrations for the rest of the school year.

It's all one thing to say in the teaching text books that violence is a call for help. It's quite another to instinctively realize it, and act upon the realization. I don't think any major universities have invited Mrs. Shackelford to be the head of their Department of Education. But that's OK. She's doing more good exactly where she is, hugging the big boys and making them pass it on.

Memoirs

*Anyone who believes you can't change history
has never tried to write his memoirs.
— David Ben Gurion*

Brown Flowers

by Anne Clarke
Christchurch, New Zealand
2004

When I was just a little girl, my Mother and Father would take me to visit Grandma Stewart. Grandma was Ellen Teresa McMillan (b. 1865, d. 1941), Irish Catholic who had eloped and married Grandfather Douglas Brown Stewart (b. 1867, d. 1928), Scottish Presbyterian.[1]

Ellen's parents had met and married in Hobart, Tasmania, Australia, on 9 February 1862.[2] They traveled to New Zealand to take part in the NZ Wars. Ellen, my grandmother, was born on 28 December 1865, in the midst of the skirmishes in the Waikato area of the North Island, New Zealand.[3]

Douglas Stewart's parents had arrived in Auckland from Glasgow in 1867, and took up land in Papakura.[4] When Robert died, Douglas bought the farm to keep it in the family, as there was still money owing on a mortgage.[5] We didn't visit Grandma very often because it was a twenty-mile journey from Auckland to Papakura—not to be taken lightly in those days. Mother would grab a long piece of wood, push it down into the petrol tank, and take a measure to see if we had sufficient fuel for the journey. The large Essex motor car we had did not have a petrol gauge. In fact, it didn't possess many instruments. It had a crank handle in the front, which my father would have to turn to start the motor. If it didn't start, he would then go to the driver's seat and fiddle with the "mixture" and try again. I guess it had a speedometer—I can't remember.

The journey to our ancestral home took over an hour. As small children, we had to crane our necks to see out of the window, because these journeys were very exciting! We took a great interest in the outside world for every inch of the trip. Most of the roads were only rough metal, but the trip down the concrete Great South Road was the highlight. The link with the south had been built during the Great Depression. It was a fine piece of road, as I remember, but, of course, the joins in the concrete always made little blips in the sound as you travelled along, not unlike the sound of a railway train on the tracks.

The open country was interspersed with small townships with their little row of shops and a church and a police station.

Our arrival at Otahuhu was always preceded by the smell wafting from the nearby Freezing Works at Westfield. The effluent from these Works was allowed to flow into the Harbour. When the tide was low, the sun on the mudflats brought out a pungent odour. We called this place, "Lavender Flats."

On arrival at the Papakura shops, Father would stop to purchase cream buns and donuts; not the donuts you buy now—they were like tennis balls covered in icing sugar, which were filled with cream and raspberry jam. Although it seemed to be an enormous paper bag, there were never enough to go around, so just a piece was all we were allowed! They were fun to eat, as you always finished up with icing sugar on the end of your nose!

From my memory, Grandma's home was a wooden house with a long front verandah. I was always filled with revulsion at the two trees at the front. They seemed quite large, and were always covered with "brown flowers." Why would Grandma want to grow trees with brown flowers? Brown flowers littered the ground. I thought they were terribly ugly.

These trees were part of the doom and gloom of the visit. On entering the kitchen, I would be told to sit on the humpty at Grandma's feet. If I was good, I would be offered a lolly later on. I remember being offered barley sugar out of a carton which had been opened and poked out of shape with hands scuffling around to remove the sticky sweets. The mantelpiece was adorned with an old clock with a beautiful picture painted on the glass panel, some strange ornaments—and the box of barley sugar. Grandma would sit in her rocking chair. Conversations would take place between Grandma, my parents, and my aunts and uncles.

My memory is of lots of legs, moon faces peering down toward me, and hair curlers. No hugs and cuddles or any personal affection was offered. As the twenty-fifth grandchild, I was no novelty, and just one of the crowd, and crowd there was. The voices were loud and had a strident tone to them. Was that because of the number of people present, each yearning to be heard among the fifteen siblings, or was it the result of them having an Irish and Scottish parentage, giving a mixed accent? I learned to sit very still, and wait for a piece of barley sugar.

This experience with Grandma is contrary to the memories of my older siblings. They say she was a lively, active person, with much fun and laughter. The family members recall the greater family arriving to celebrate Christmas, pitching their tents, and enjoying great parties. By the time I was born, this "old lady," my Grandmother, was worn out having reared fifteen children alone. Grandfather worked in Auckland, and only visited the farm at the weekends.

I found out that the trees with brown flowers were camellia trees, one being red and the other white. I never saw that colour. I also understand that there was an impressive front garden. Was it still there when I was a child, or had time taken its toll on the plot? Perhaps my attention was taken up with the brown flowers on the trees!

I do not like camellias—one look, and all I see are the brown flowers. They remind me of the colourless sepia-like relationship I had with my widowed Grandmother. Grandma died when I was seven years of age.[6]

RESOURCES

1. *Marriage Register*, District of Auckland, New Zealand, 30 April 1886.

2. *Marriage Register*, District of Huon, Tasmania, Australia, 9 February 1862.

3. Birth Registration, District of Cambridge, Waikato, New Zealand, 28 December 1865.

4. *Rate Book*, Papakura Council Records, 1888.

5. *Rate Book*, Papakura Council Records, 1897.

6. Cemetery Records, Papakura Council, 11 October, 1941.

LEGACY

Amy W. Falkenstein
Fairmont, West Virginia
2004

There are two vivid memories of when I was young: one, Granddaddy, and two, the late-night car rides to Myrtle Beach each summer in our Oldsmobile station wagon with tinted windows. But especially Granddaddy. He was the last of the Southern gentlemen, my mom always said. He moved to Fairmont, West Virginia, at age nineteen, hours and cultures away from his family farm in Schuyler, Virginia, where he made a mere $18 a year as a farmer. He wore a brown felt hat, always, and a trench coat and nodded to ladies in public, even to my sister, Lori, and me. We through he looked terribly sophisticated. I think the reason for the hat was to protect his round and shiny bald head, not for the sake of image. In his top dresser drawer, he kept sticks of Doublemint chewing gum for Lori and me.

Often, in autumn, he'd come down with pneumonia, and the house was uncannily quiet when he was sick. I'd sneak into his and Memama's dim bedroom and crawl atop the warm, hard bed next to him.

"Hey, Good Lookin'," he'd smile, toothless. It always made me laugh when he didn't have his teeth in. Sometimes, when he wasn't coughing too badly, I'd curl up and lay my head on his bony shoulder. I'd drink in the familiar smells of Vicks VapoRub and instant coffee, listening to the soft gurgle of the dehumidifier.

In summers, since Granddad and Memama lived only six houses down the street from us, I'd spend the days on their backporch swing, snapping and stringing green beans from their big garden. Memama would be clanking around in the kitchen, baking bread for Sunday morning when the whole entire family visited them after church. We'd get to snack on homemade bread (drenched in butter, toasted on the griddle) or peanut butter and Saltine crackers, or, signifying a special occasion, apple float, a foamy and mysteriously pink concoction—perhaps akin to, or a hybrid of, applesauce, an Orange Julius, and sand. My cousins and Lori and I read the Sunday comics sprawled out on the floor, and then swung on the front porch swing until, getting into trouble because of banging the swing against the house, we'd form a line on the living room couch and scratch each other's backs while our parents gave commentary on the usual boring subjects: weather, the preacher's sermon that morning, and an occasional political issue.

Granddaddy smiled widely, relaxed in his reupholstered recliner (Memama did it herself, by the way), with a mug of Sanka coffee that read, "I love grandpa," with a smiley face on it.

The call came as a surprise, fifteen years later, although it shouldn't have. After all, Granddaddy's health had been seriously failing, especially since Memama's death a few years before. We had adjusted, by default, to silent Sunday mornings. Mom even learned to make oatmeal cookies from scratch—Memama's recipe—but it clearly wasn't the same.

I clutched him as he lay in the casket in the stale, cold funeral home. Coffee was brewing somewhere, muffled sobbing around me. I laid my head against his lifeless forehead, my hair covering his face and chest; I was shaking. The world had lost its last Southern gentleman. I could swear I smelled Vicks as my cheek pressed against his. I was getting us both wet with my tears, and hands from nowhere were trying to pull me away as the preacher assured me I'd see him in Heaven one day.

Was that supposed to help me at the moment?

Defeated, I allowed myself to be withdrawn, tears silently dripping from my face as I was led out of the building and into the orange October sunshine. The earth emanated autumn's fresh scent of leaves, dead, crunchy, and brittle, on the sidewalks, lawns, and roadways. Beautiful and savory, but dead: West Virginia's bittersweet irony.

I dozed on the back deck on my mom's favorite wicker loveseat, exhausted. I drank coffee and tried to chat politely with friends from out of town, but invariably I drifted to sleep in the rusty afternoon sun. Eventually, when I awoke, everyone had shuffled inside for strawberry pie from Shoney's, a condolence gift from the ladies in the Bereavement Ministries at church. I lay on the shadowy, flowered deck alone.

At length, Mom came out to check on me. "Can't you come in and be friendly?"

She was the perfect hostess, despite tragedy or death. She was a carbon copy of Memama herself, a prim and proper and altogether headstrong redhead. I knew, though, she would be hurting later, in privacy, when the guests were gone. I wasn't as good at checking my emotions as she.

"I tried," I choked, wiping my eyes roughly, my pain anew. "I did, honest." She patted my panty-hosed knee and quietly closed the screen door behind her on the way back inside. A woman's incessant chatter came from a distance, and someone asked Mom if I was OK.

Life changed for me that day, the day I experienced the worst pain of my entire twenty-six-year existence. It was actually refreshing, believe it or not, because with this pain came the realization that I would never have to suffer the loss of my grandfather again. It was, thankfully, a one-time deal. I learned that I was strong, anoth-

136

er refreshing realization.

Now, six years later, I'm teaching my son to be a gentleman, to like green beans, to dig in the garden, to be strong. He's two-and-a-half-years old, and several times a week, we walk by Memama and Granddaddy's old house, the porch swing gone and a bay window in its place, but the peeling white kitchen shutters still miraculously intact. This is an easy and sensible activity for us, seeing as how we live only one street over, my son the fourth generation to live in the small and relatively quiet neighborhood of Bellview, a mere minute or so away from downtown Fairmont. The leaves have already turned and fallen, and in the past two years, they've been gorgeous.

THE BODIES
IN THE BASEMENT

By Bonnie Copeland
Costa Mesa, California
2004

T he bodies were kept in our basement, lined up hip to hip on plain wooden shelves. All of Grandma's regular clients had bodies. So did my Mother and Aunt Leah and all the relatives that Grandma liked. None of the relatives Grandma disliked had bodies because she didn't want to do work for them. I didn't have one because I grew too fast.

Some people had many bodies. Grandma never let the clients go down to the basement to see the brutal history of their lives morphing from slender flexible youth to the heavy collapse of middle age. She did, however, keep her own old bodies on a shelf behind the ironing board where she could view and comment on them while she pressed other people's clothes.

"Ah, look at dat vaist," she said wistfully. "It grew von inch bigger efery year I vas married. Ven I was seventeen, Papa could put two hands around it und die fingers vould touch!"

The price of making a custom body was $25 in 1948, the equivalent of $175 in 2005. Only wealthy clients could pay for them. Bodies saved time, and time was money for these ladies. Women who bought bodies did not have to stand for hours while Grandma draped their figures and cut patterns for new clothes out of heavy cotton muslin fabric. Owning a body distilled the client's part in the dressmaking process to the fun: choosing a style from a photograph or sketch, debating about fabric, trim, and finishing. The body did the donkey work. It didn't complain. It showed up and stood still while Grandma tugged and pinned the garment into shape.

Grandmother liked to make a new body whenever someone gained or lost more than ten pounds or aged five years. The prospect of a new body was a powerful weapon in the war against telling the truth about your age or getting fat. Women who had once been through the body-making process would do almost anything to avoid experiencing it again.

Bodies were made out of papier-maché, from strips of newspaper dipped in flour-and-water glue. Sometimes the thin papier-maché itself became the core of the mannequin, sometimes the shell was used as a mold for plaster.

We always made bodies on Saturday so that my dad was home to help. We started saving newspapers about two weeks before the appointment. Dad and I were in charge of tearing the paper into narrow strips and stacking them neatly in a laundry basket. On the morning of the event, dad draped oilcloth over the carpeted fitting platform and the Oriental rug and carried several buckets of warm water up the stairs to the workroom. He dissolved flour into one of the buckets and stirred it into a watery, sticky glue. Then he moved the samovar from the buffet in the dining room to the mahogany dresser in the workroom and filled it with hot coals, water, and tea.

The client was instructed to wear the brassiere and girdle she planned to use with the new garment and her oldest slip and to arrive early. Grandma usually spent a few minutes in social chat on the sofa with each lady, catching up on life over tea and cookies, but not on body days! "No ticky-talk today," she announced as she marched the lady up the stairs. "Let's get it over vit!"

The client stood on the fitting platform while Grandma wrapped her in damp newspaper strips, round and round. Between layers they gossiped over tea from the samovar. As each layer dried, Grandma added another to the wet shell. Entombed for hours from thigh to neck, the client shivered and drank tea, shivered and drank tea.

By noon the shell was stiff and itchy and dry enough to stand on its own. Grandma neatly inserted a sharp scissors with blades like a duck's bill and cut through cast and slip on one side of the form, thigh to underarm, leaving the bra and girdle intact. Then she sliced across one shoulder so that the client could slide out. Instead of stepping into the warmed robe Grandma held open for her, the newly liberated client always ran down the hall in her bra and girdle.

"Ahhh," we would hear from behind the bathroom door, "ahhh."

After the client left, Grandma put the cut papier-maché body between the two workroom windows to dry in the sun. When it was dry enough, Grandma zipped it together with more papier-maché and sanded it slightly smaller than the client's measurements. Dad painted it with several coats of shellac so it wouldn't soften, and Grandma wrapped it with a thin layer of lambs wool that she could push pins into. She hand fitted and sewed a natural linen cover that smoothed the rough spots and placed seams and darts exactly where they would go in a finished garment.

The final step was a somber one. Dad lifted the client's old body off of its stand and replaced it with the new one. Then he raised the old body to his shoulder and, trailed by Grandmother and me, carried it out of the workroom, past the stained glass window that threw butterfly lights onto the carpeted stairs to the first floor, through the hall, and down the rickety steps to its final resting place on the plain wooden shelves in the basement.

A Shepherd Hears
the Angels' Song

by Diane Kolb
Melrose Park, Pennsylvania
2004

19 53: Twenty pairs of Buster Browns could be seen swinging back and forth on the large wooden chairs in the Sunday School room. Miss April, the pageant director, fluttered about handing out piles of typewritten pages to various parent helpers. This was the moment everyone had been waiting for. The parts for the Christmas Pageant were to be announced.

I held my breath as Miss April walked with measured steps down the row of children. Maybe this would be the year I would get to be an angel. I could just see myself in the shimmering, blue junior choir robe with the white tissue-paper wings spread out behind me like a great white bird. The hanger twisted to fit like a halo and covered with aluminum foil would sit on top of my Dutch boy hair cut sparkling in the candlelight.

At age seven, I had been in the Sunday School Christmas Pageant four years running. I had played every part except an angel. I even made an appearance one year as a sheep when there were too many children and not enough parts to go around.

I folded my hands together so tightly my knuckles turned white. The flowered dress stopped in front of my chair. "Short, dark hair . . ." Miss April mumbled to herself. "Diane, you will make a fine shepherd," she said sweetly looking down at me. Then she smiled, patted my head, and moved on to the next child.

I couldn't believe it. I was relegated to the burlap brigade again; scratchy bathrobe, kitchen-towel head scarf, and wooden walking stick. I was stuck with all the boys again! Hot tears were already welling up in my eyes and I kept my head down and bit my lip so no one would see my disappointment. When all the parts were assigned, I raised my head and snuck a peek down the row of children. Every little girl with pretty, long, blonde hair was already in the costume box, sizing up their blue robes and trying on halos.

All the shepherds were led to a corner and given our ragbag outfits. The boys had a lot of fun at my expense, joking about me being "one of the fellas." I wanted to crawl under my chair and disappear. I was always taught never to argue with a grown-up and to do what I was told without comment, so I spoke to no one and followed the director's staging. (Even though, after a couple of years in the same part, I had become an expert at being "sore afraid.")

When the rehearsal was finally over, the sun made long shadows on the pavement and I had to hurry to be home before dark. I grabbed the dreaded sackcloth costume and stuffed it in a brown bag and ran for the door. The air felt sharp and cold on my face as I raced up the side driveway, my face still flaming after facing such a humiliation. One of my mittens was among the missing, so I curled my fingers around the brown bag to keep them warm as I hurried down the two blocks to my house.

The warm, dry air wrapped around my shivering body like a blanket. I could smell the aroma of sauerkraut and pork coming from the kitchen and my mouth watered. I didn't realize how hungry I was. There were freshly baked Christmas cookies cooling on newspaper on the dining room table. Everything was just perfect—except for me.

I thought I could escape unseen, but my mother was too clever for me. She must have seen me from the kitchen out of the corner of her eye, and came out to greet me wiping her hands on the towel draped over her shoulder. When I saw her bright smile and out-stretched arms, the tears came out of nowhere, and I collapsed in her arms.

"What is it, sweetheart? What's the matter?" she asked.

Without looking directly at her, I explained what had happened between short breaths. "I'm a shepherd again, Mom," I said through tears. "When do I get to be an angel? It's not fair! Just because I don't have yellow hair! Didn't God make any angels with brown hair?"

"Of course He did," she said, gathering me into her lap. "Angels come in all shapes and sizes, and their hair can be any color at all. They're all around us. And every once in a while on Christmas Eve, if you listen very carefully, you can hear them singing."

"Aw, that's just a story," I said, running my finger across my dripping nose.

"Hmmm, very possibly. But a good one!" she said with a wink. She pulled a handkerchief from her apron and wiped my face with it. "There," she said. "Dry your eyes. The most important thing you can do now is be the best shepherd you can be. After all, the pageant has lots of children in it all trying to do their best to make it a success. What do you say? Want to give it a try?" I agreed.

When Christmas Eve arrived, it was gray and frosty outside, and there was talk around the breakfast table of a white Christmas. That added excitement to our day. Snow was definitely in the air.

The day passed painfully slowly until Mom announced it was time to get ready for the Christmas Pageant. My costume was pressed and ready for me on a wire hanger. I washed my face and combed my short hair. Mom let me wear my Sunday dress, even though it wasn't Sunday. She said tonight was a special night and deserved a special dress. Mom's eyes glistened as she hugged me and helped me on with my heavy winter coat. It was only four o'clock, but the sky was already dark and gray. I had to go early. The rest of the family would come later. With my costume over my arm, I walked up the hill to the church.

The cast was all assembled and lined up in order of our appearance in the play. The narrator went on stage first and the audience got still. The story of the first Christmas was read from the Bible and presented like a tableau. Christmas carols were sung here and there during the presentation. When the reader got to the part about the shepherds, I proudly took my place and did my best to look "sore afraid."

The boys had left their burlap robes crumpled in the brown bags all week. Mine was the only one pressed and neat. My mother had told me I would stand out in the group and she would be very proud of me. I never took my eyes off her.

When the Pageant was over, there were refreshments for all and even a visit from Santa Claus. Each of us got a small box of hard candy with a candy cane on top. It was the first gift of Christmas. As we left the church for our short walk home, the snow began to fall. Snow on Christmas Eve! What could be more wonderful!

After dinner, my sisters and I decorated the tree with our paper stars, hung the stockings, and got ourselves ready for bed. There were no outside storm windows to keep out the winter wind, but upstairs, it was warm and steamy from each of us taking our bath one after another.

As I lay in my small bed with my baby sister asleep in the crib on the opposite side of the room, I thought of how this Christmas was almost perfect. Mom helped me be the best shepherd. I knew she was proud of me. The snow was already falling and had coated everything with a blanket of white. It was the best Christmas ever and it no longer mattered to me that I never got to be an angel.

From my window, I could see the lights at the top of the Fireproof Storage building if I stooped way down. They made an orange glow on the floor. I liked to sneak out of bed at night, raise the faded shade, sit in that spotlight and pretend I was on a stage. It was late and the house was quiet. Then it happened. I heard voices outside. Music. I thought at first I was imagining it. It seemed to be coming from far away. Could it be? Were the angels really singing?

I tiptoed over to the window. If I opened it, the blast of cold air would certainly wake the baby. So I scratched the ice off of a small area, and pressed my ear to the window. The sound I heard was the most beautiful singing I had ever heard in my life. Not just voices, but trumpets and other instruments. I stayed there listening as long as my now-frozen ear could stand it.

I remembered what my mother told me about hearing the angels sing on Christmas Eve if you listened very hard. She was right again. The angels were singing for me! "Halleluia!" they sang over and over with the sound of trumpets and violins. It was the best Christmas present I ever got or ever will get again.

I never told a soul what I heard that night. It was my own treasure.

Many years later I found an explanation for what might have happened that night. I was asked to write an article for the church newsletter about our old church building.

The tower originally housed bells, but they were sold during the Civil War to buy medicine for the soldiers. After that, the only music that ever came from the tower was from the speakers that were put up there during World War II. At Christmas and Easter, the custodian would put on records of choirs singing hymns and it would broadcast from the speakers in the tower to the neighborhood. When I visited the tower, Handel's *Messiah* sat on the top of a pile of dusty 78s. It all came flooding back to me.

Could that have been the singing I heard? It is a reasonable explanation, but it just doesn't ring true to me. No evidence in the world can take away the memory of a little girl who truly believes, even after all these years, that her mother somehow arranged to have the angels sing just for her that snowy Christmas Eve.

Serendipity

The difference between fiction and reality?
Fiction has to make sense.
— Tom Clancy

BEHIND THE WALLS
OF FOLSOM PRISON

by Dennis McCargar
Tujunga, California
2002

I was the senior law librarian at New Folsom Prison (California State Penitentiary-Sacramento) for nearly seven years, 1995-2002. My first week on the job, I visited the Folsom Prison Museum, which has an intriguing display of artifacts, handmade inmate weapons, mug books, a model of an early cell, newspaper accounts of escapes, photos of former wardens, an album of executions by hanging, and a photo of the prison cemetery.

That last one really captured my attention, and I soon discovered that little was known about the cemetery. There were no records of prison burials. Some graves had stone markers, but most displayed only a prison number from an old numbering scheme no longer in use—no name, no date. Many graves have only a wood stake for a marker, with few legible notations. I soon met with the museum president, who commissioned me, as a volunteer, to compile a checklist of burials, needed to respond to frequent calls to the prison about former prisoners, most of which were referred to the museum and went unanswered.

Over the next six years, I tallied the few records that had penciled notations of death, often just the single word, "dead." None included the place of burial. I toured the cemetery, making a map and numbering the gravesites, noting every scrap of data on stone and stake alike. I examined prison records in the museum, and local newspapers for death notices and escape accounts. I examined records at the State Archives, the San Quentin Prison Museum, the Sacramento County Archives, local cemeteries and crematoriums, the state hospitals at Napa and Stockton (formerly called asylums), and the Sacramento County Clerk's office. I lived at the clerk's office for better than two years on my days off. County death records confirmed and augmented the sparse details I had collected.

It had been estimated that there were about five hundred inmate burials in the prison cemetery, but my checklist grew to over 1,100 deaths, with prison burials confirmed for about eight hundred, from county records. The last burial was in 1959, rather than 1955, as I had been told. The present location was the third move of a cemetery that began on the bluffs of the American River, where it sometimes washed away in spring floods. Some remains were recovered down river and reinterred, but many had been lost to high water, and more were lost from the successive moves until reaching the last grassy hillside. Many more than first estimated were buried or reinterred off grounds by family members.

Sometime in 1997, as I was collecting inmate aliases that were added in pencil, I found the name William Jesse Hogan, an alias for Matthew J. Murphy, who died in 1920, and was buried at the prison. This name set off an alarm, because my mother's grandfather, by the same name, had disappeared in 1896 from the Missouri Ozarks.

I have spent the better part of forty years researching my father's family, without ever tackling my mother's side. She always said that it was a dead end: Her father was orphaned, and her mother was the only child born in this country of a German immigrant family.

148

A few months before I saw that name in the list of inmate aliases, my uncle, Mom's older brother, had sent me the results of his inquiries into the Hogan family, providing great-grandfather's name, and the revised story of his having abandoned a young and pregnant wife, who gave up her son to an older, barren sister. That son, my Grandpa, had "orphaned himself," when he learned that the man who had been beating him regularly was not his father. He left that home at thirteen, never meeting either parent.

The more I looked at Murphy/Hogan, the more I began to think that he really might be my long-lost great-grandfather. Once I found his death certificate, and various court records from California and Nevada, all doubt was erased. His railroading background, education, birth in Kentucky and family home in Missouri, his physical descriptions and mug shots, all seemed to prove the theory. And, he resembles my grandfather Hogan, the son he never knew.

His criminal record consisted of several busts for second-degree burglary, always rewarded with a short prison term. From court records, I learned that he was well-educated, but had become a drunk. He would stay sober and save his earnings for months, then go on a binge, drinking up the savings, then making a feeble attempt to steal something, to maintain the liquor flow. He always got caught. He was more of a danger to himself than to others.

Hogan/Murphy died in the prison hospital, April 2, 1920, four years before my mother was born. I have placed flowers on his grave every April since 1997, and I am confident that the only other flowers to grace that spot are the wild California poppies that adorn the hillside cemetery every spring.

A word about inmates. Time and again it has been proven that an ex-convict is less likely to repeat his crime or crimes if, upon parole, he stays with, or stays in close touch with, his family. Recognizing that a family historian needs both plenty of time and a closer relationship with older family members, to get started, I volunteered to teach a beginning genealogy class for inmates, who *needed* to reestablish family contacts. I have had great success, and never better than when I confessed to a class of inmates that my great-grandfather rests in the Folsom Prison Cemetery. Suddenly, I was one of them, a "homey." Suddenly, I had the rapt attention and respect of my listeners, and the questions never stopped. Many of those men remain committed to producing something of value for their families: a family tree.

The work on the Cemetery Project has ground to a halt since my retirement and return to Southern California. I'll finish it, but my original thought to provide a resource for other family researchers has already borne lots of fruit—and, unexpectedly, a plum for me.

My Turned-to-the-Wall
Great-Grandfather

by Marian Bailey Presswood
Benton, Tennessee
2003

Like a lot of folks out there, I'm afraid I waited until everyone who could have told me about my family history was long gone. Too busy getting an education as an older student, caring for a family while doing so, and then teaching for many years, didn't leave a whole lot of time for root searching.

And then, one day in 1990, with big tears in his eyes, my ninety-three-year-old Dad lamented the sad fact that he had not been interested when his mother and sisters were discussing family, and now they were all gone and he had no one to ask. Being an educator with the summer off, I decided to tackle the task of finding something for Dad about his family.

When asked if he had pictures of any of his grandparents, he instructed me to remove the large framed picture from the wall in front of him. Puzzled, I did so, glancing at the words "Lillard Hardware Company" that appeared at the top of the scene of the beautiful old country house captured in the moonlight—a familiar picture during all my childhood years in that old farmhouse.

Dad took out his pocket knife and carefully pried loose the small tacks holding the backing, and removed the picture, turning it around—and there was my great-grandfather John M. Griffith, smiling at me with his bright blue eyes![1] Mom came into the room about that time and explained: "I didn't know that old man with the big hands, and I didn't like him staring at me all the time, so I turned him toward the wall and pasted me a pretty picture on the back!"

After making copies of the picture of my newly discovered great-grandfather, I began to quiz Dad about any information he could remember hearing of his family. Dad was born October 19, 1897, and was only two years old when his father died in February 1900, so he had no recollection of how he looked. Since he seemed more interested in his beloved mother, Zilpha Jane Griffith's, family, that's where we started.

The picture was of Zilpha's father, but Dad knew little to nothing about the father's parents or siblings, nor those of his wife, Jane Ann Rogers. He did happen to remember that he took his mother to visit one of her sisters out on Sand Mountain, Alabama, once or twice in the early 1930s, so that's where I headed.

Being a brand new researcher, I was extremely ignorant of all the resources available—and, in fact, had never even seen a census on microfilm. It didn't even occur to me to go to a library, and I probably wouldn't have had the foggiest notion what to do when I got there, anyway. My thought was to just go to the area, look up any Griffith names in the phone book, call and explain who I was and ask if they knew any of the names that my Dad had mentioned as belonging to our family.

What followed was nothing short of a miracle, as I look back on it from my current knowledge of the Internet, censuses, vital statistics, and all the other resources available to today's researchers.

The very first phone call turned out to be to a descendant of Dad's Aunt Susanna Griffith Ledford, who graciously invited me to their home, shared family pictures—some were even old tintypes—

and took me to all the area cemeteries. I was totally unprepared for my reaction to the last picture they wanted to show me, which was hanging in their bedroom. It was the same picture of my great-grandfather that my Mom had turned toward the wall at our house many years ago. Through misty eyes, I whispered, "Hello again, Great-Grandfather Griffith."

That one summer, I learned the names of every one of my Dad's maternal aunts and uncles, their children, and for the most part, when they died and where they were buried. Dad was able to travel with me to many of the cemeteries, and knelt at the final resting places of relatives he never had the opportunity to meet during their lifetime.

By this time, I had decided to try my luck at the Fannin County, Georgia, courthouse to see if there was a will or deed, since we had no clue as to the location of their old homeplace. Receiving the usual, "courthouse burned, no records" reply from the elected officials, for some reason, I lingered a moment and reached down to the bottom shelf and picked up a small, well-worn ledger that was labeled, "miscellaneous." Flipping through just to see what kind of records it contained, out jumped the Griffith name—an 1863 will of my grand-grandfather, and a long list of items sold at "public outcry" after my great-great-grandparents died in the mid-1850s. Although Dad thought their name was Rodgers, I hadn't even known their given names, Hugh and Anna, until that moment.

While we were on one of our outings to visit new-found relatives and explore cemeteries, Dad mentioned an old friend he would like to see, and we stopped at a little white frame house beside a North Georgia mountain road. The friend, Lawrence Stanley, had written several little books on the history and people of Fannin and Cilmer counties in Georgia, and I purchased a couple for Dad.

Looking back, it was more than a coincidence—serendipity, if you will—that we did so. For later, while reading the book, Dad discovered a short excerpt about a Civil War skirmish involving Georgia Home Guards, in which his grandfather, John M. Griffith, was shot and later died. It was the same month as his will was written, June 1863. The article triggered almost-lost memories, and Dad was able to recall some of the stories he had heard from his mother about the horrors of the events that happened during that awful war. The pieces of the family puzzle were at long last beginning to form a discernable picture.

The story about great-grandfather's death mentioned Persimmon Creek and described the terrain, which Dad recognized as being at the junction of Big Creek and the Toccoa River in Fannin County, Georgia. Our next outing was planned to explore that area, and again, we really lucked out by meeting the owner of the little campground right at the very spot where we were to cross the river.

Herman Long and Dad discovered that between the two of them, they knew every family that had lived in those mountains for the last seventy-five years! I thought they would never wind down enough for us to cross the river to the old homeplace, but they finally did, and Mr. Long graciously provided the boat that transported us to the other side—and we stepped out on "holy ground"! Deep in Chattahoochie National Forest, the old chimney was still standing, and part of the garden rock wall, and even a little cemetery that we later learned contained the graves of some infants.

In retrospect, it seems to me that even though I was totally ignorant of all the genealogy resources that might have been available, I did exactly the right thing by starting with my own father to begin my family research.

I then sought out any other relatives who might add to this information, and I visited cemeteries, courthouses, and libraries. A little over ten years later, I'm the official county historian for Polk County, Tennessee, reorganizer and ten-year president of a four-hundred-member historical society, editor of an award-winning quarterly newsletter, and head librarian of our little genealogy library.

Through these positions, I come in contact with hundreds of researchers who are seeking to preserve their family histories. However, I am constantly amazed that in many cases, those researchers have relied almost totally on the Internet, and have little or no experience in obtaining oral family history, or digging through dusty old courthouse records. Many won't even bother reading microfilmed records. If it doesn't come as easy as a click of the mouse, forget it.

While none of this is meant as criticism of our wonderful technological innovations that have opened doors to so many who would not otherwise have the opportunity to do research, I do think many people are missing a lot by limiting their research to the Internet, with all its errors and misinformation. It might be time to get back to the basics, and learn how to locate original records, and become familiar with where they're stored in your county.

After all, would I have ever found my turned-to-the-wall Great-Grandfather Griffith on the Internet? Not in my lifetime!

RESOURCES

1. *The portrait was apparently enlarged from a tintype, and had been tinted and his blue eyes just stood out. This has been a "big thing" in my family as long as I can remember: "You weren't a Bailey unless you had blue eyes."*

ECHOES

By *William Lewis Principe, Jr.*
La Canada Flintridge, California
2004

It is a radiant summer day in my step-daughter Sheila's backyard in Hopedale, Massachusetts. The foliage on the trees is that familiar shade of intense dark green that densely covers New England trees in July. Through the leaves I can barely make out the Mill River rippling across the rear of Sheila's property, and just beyond it is Hartford Street. Her husband, Jay, is mowing the lawn in their yard, which is edged by those low 17-Century rock walls, laid by hand and with no mortar, that line the New England countryside.

On the table next to me are two old and yellowing 19th-Century maps of the town of Milford. Studying these maps sends chills down my back. I am not a superstitious man, but every now and then something transpires that transcends rational explanation, and these mundane maps offer a startling example. How could this have happened? As I study the maps, I hear Sheila's car pull into the driveway, and I squirm in my chair, in the anticipation of sharing my discovery with her . . .

Like many people who are drawn to genealogy later in life, I grew up knowing little about my ancestry. Both of my parents were estranged from their extended families, and I had met few relatives beyond my grandparents. It wasn't until a distant cousin, dying of cancer, opened up to me that I finally found the key that unlocked the hazy mystery of my heritage.

"Lewis," he said, "Lewis," and then I knew my grandmother's surname. Like strands of DNA in my cells, I had been carrying the code to my ancestry in my own middle name, Lewis, without ever knowing it; Over the next few years, diligent research would bring a flood of surnames, which today are as familiar to me as if I had known them all my life: Lewis, Tillinghast, Grant, Reynolds, Albee; and on the more-recent immigrant sides of my family, Barraco, da Silva, and Albin.

I now know Benjamin Albee to have been my eighth great-grandfather. In 1642, he became a freeman in Braintree, but something in the air of that Massachusetts town disagreed with him and he soon moved to Medfield (1649), Mendon (1664), and then Milford, where in 1665 he built the first water-powered grist mill in Worcester County,[1] an outpost of civilization in what was then the Wild West. But toward the end of his life, Indians and King Phillip's War drove him east again, and he finally died in Swansea, Massachusetts, the progenitor of families, including mine, who would spread across southeast Massachusetts and Rhode Island and, ultimately, to California.

Nineteenth-Century published genealogies describe the site of Benjamin's corn mill as being near "what is now the Lewis B. Gaskill place,"[2] so I had hoped that studying old maps might show me the mill's exact location. It was those maps, found at the Milford Public Library, that so thrilled me as I sat on Sheila's back porch. One of them, drawn about 1898,[3] showed the names of property owners throughout Milford and Hopedale, and there, to my delight, where Hartford Street crosses the Mill River, I had found L. B. Gaskill. The other map, torn and tattered and a hundred years older,[4] was even more definitive, for it showed "Alby's Corn Mill" just across the river at the same spot.

In the middle of the 19th-Century, a group of utopians led by Adin Ballou had settled in western Milford. They soon split away from that town's government and formed a new town reflecting their optimism and aspirations, which they named Hopedale.[5] More than a century later, Sheila and Jay would buy a home on a quiet cul-de-sac in that part of old Milford that had become Hopedale, along the Mill River near Hartford Street.

And that, it turns out, was the source of those chills down my back, for my maps showed that three hundred-forty years after Benjamin Albee built the grist mill that gave the Mill River its name, my own family would unknowingly settle in the very same spot, along the Mill River near Hartford Street. Was it karma? Or do coincidences defy calculation? But this coincidence was only the most recent of several I had discovered in my quest for family.

As a young man, my brother, Steve, had left our native California to join friends at Berwick, Maine, where he worked as a bar-keep in a local pub. When he told me the name of the town, it sounded exotic, as tantalizing as Bora Bora or Madras. But then genealogy brought it into focus, and years later I discovered that our ancestor, the Scotsman Peter Grant, had lived there.[6] In 1650, Grant was captured by Oliver Cromwell's army of Roundheads at the Battle of Dunbar,[7,8] and, along with many other defeated Scottish soldiers, he was exiled to the far-off Massachusetts Bay Colony, as a slave in the Saugus Iron Works, the first industrial establishment in the entire New World.[9] Seven years later, he won his freedom by his drudgery and sweat and removed north to the Piscataqua River, where he claimed property in Berwick. Three hundred-twenty years after that, before he had ever heard of Grant or Saugus or distant Anglo-Scottish wars, Steve moved 3,000 miles, to a house less than three hundred yards from his ninth great-grandfather Peter's homestead.[10] Why had Steve's peregrinations taken him to Berwick?

As a young man, I had fled to New York City to seek the unbounded excitement that I missed in the quiet suburbs of our native California. I rented an apartment on East 11th Street in the

East Village, surrounded by hippies, artists, and Ukranian immigrants, for whom the neighborhood had a grittier name, the Lower East Side. Years later, my family research would tell me that in the building next door to where I had lived, sixty years earlier, my grandfather Morris Albin had sought a new life away from the *schtetls* of his native Ukraine.[11] Why had I traveled 3,000 miles to live thirty paces from my grandfather, whose name I did not know then, and whose photograph I still have not been able to find?

So there they are: coincidences that defy computation. To me, it doesn't seem possible that these events, separated by thousands of miles and hundreds of years, could have happened simply by chance. Perhaps, as in my DNA and my middle name, there is something encoded into those places that calls to me and my family. Perhaps there is such a thing as inherited memory; perhaps key words such as Berwick, Ukraine, or Milford echo down to me, passed silently from generation to generation. And perhaps echoes like these ring down through all families, a natural part of the fabric of life and descendancy.

● Three hundred-forty years later, my step-daughter unknowingly buys the acre that my eighth great-grandfather cleared for his mill, leaving her the legacy of the low and graceful stone walls that surround her yard.

● Three hundred-twenty years later, my brother moves across the continent to a neighborhood that he could not have possibly known was once home to our ninth great-grandfather, and drives his motorcycle down the same winding roads where our ancestor once drove his livestock.

● Sixty years later, I hitch-hike across the continent to live next door to my grandfather's tenement, each of us finding freedom in those grimy, raucous streets from different sets of bounds.

. . . As Sheila parks the car and walks out onto the porch, I prepare the tattered maps for her, anxious to share my discovery. We sit together, and I point out into the backyard to the spot where Benjamin Albee ground his corn in 1665. We talk about the ancient walls that

run down to the river, and about the remnants of the mill dam still visible in the water.

Sheila is clearly impressed, but genealogy, like youth, is often wasted on the young, and soon the conversation turns to grandsons and groceries and more modern matters, leaving me to feel my shivers alone. But as I stare out into the yard on this humid July afternoon, I am certain I glimpse Benjamin Albee carefully stacking stones around his field, as Jay mows his grass. Centuries may separate us, but we're still family.

REFERENCES

1. Adin Ballou, _History of the town of Milford, Worcester County, Massachusetts; from its first settlement to 1881_ (Boston: Franklin Press, 1882), 522 ff.

2. Ibid., p. 35.

3. _Map of Milford, Massachusetts_ (c. 1898?), in collection of Milford Public Library. This map shows the L. B. Gaskill property on Hartford Street, just west of the Mill River.

4. _Map of Milford, Massachusetts_ (c. 1800?), in collection of Milford Public Library. This map shows "Alby's Corn Mill" on Hartford Street, just west of the Mill River. Of course, the mill dam would have spanned the river, and the mill itself would have included land on both shores.

5. Anon., _Dedication of the Adin Ballou memorial_ (Cambridge: Riverside Press, 1901)

6. Leola Grant Bushman. _Peter Grant, Scotch exile: Kittery and Berwick, Maine._ (San Marino, CA: self-published, 1971-76).

7. Stuart Reid. _Scots Armies of the English Civil Wars_ (Botley, Oxfordshire: Osprey Publishing, 1999), p. 9.

8. Jon G. McLennan, _Ridge of Tears_ (Bishop, CA: 1980), pp. 34-6.

9. Anon., _The Saugus Ironworks Restoration_ (Saugus: Eastern National, 1999).

10. Anon. _Map of the Property Grant to James Warren by the Selectmen of Kittery_, July 15, 1656, in collection of Maine Historical Society. This map shows a narrow strip of land belonging to "Peter Grant, 31 Oct 1659," which ran from Grant's Point on the shore of the Salmon Falls (Piscataqua) River to present-day Route 103, where Steve lived in the 1970s.

11. Morris Albin, _Naturalization Petition_ (New York County Supreme Court: 17 Dec 1907). In his petition, Morris gives his birthplace as Buczacz, a schtetl (village) in present-day Ukraine, and his current address as 551 E. 11th Street. In 1966 I had lived at 547 E. 11th Street.

MARGARET'S TRIUMPH

by Emily Pritchard Cary
Scottsdale, Arizona
2001

Start with a national relic, stir in a restless spirit, add a dollop of parapsychology, season with an inexplicable journey, and serve it up on a rare day in June. *Voila!* The concoction is Margaret's triumph!

Steely-eyed and prim, Margaret Forster Steuart regarded me throughout my adolescence. Whenever I recall those growing-up years in Swarthmore, Pennsylvania, she is the first feature of our house that comes to mind. Funny that she should have given me pause, for she was only a portrait.

With glance averted, I approached the top of the staircase where she dominated the wall, prodding me with those dark, piercing eyes, stern and uncompromising in mien. No matter that Mother extolled her virtues as a famous ancestor, I regarded her as one might an eerie, extra-natural spirit pervading the dark hallway, bent on fingering me for her own arcane purposes.

Mother laughed off my pleas to remove Margaret from sight,

reminding me, "She made Perry's flag, 'Don't Give Up The Ship.' You should be very proud of your great-great grandmother."

I felt no communion with the art gallery of naval officers and battleships flanking Margaret, which my mother, a latent historian, had mounted along the wall. Whenever an unsuspecting guest inquired about the collection (and even when they didn't), Mother took pleasure in narrating our family history. The ancestral tree included a veritable Army (and Navy) of early Pennsylvania pioneers, the least comely of whom was surely Margaret.

Two decades after being separated from the sobriety of suburban Philadelphia, I moved to Fairfax, Virginia, near Washington, D. C. By then I had forgotten Margaret, whose features were now out of sight in the thick volume of family history that had become officially mine through the finality of inheritance. Little did I suspect that she was about to break through that fine line separating reality from the extra-sensory. Blame it on my psychic friend.

Far more than a self-professed psychic, Jackie Altisi is a practitioner of the ancient art of clairaudience, or hearing beyond sounds discernible to mortal man. Her two decades of volunteer service to government organizations searching for new angles on unexplained phenomena led her to the ESP Laboratory of the United Nations, where her classes attracted representatives from many countries seeking mutual enlightenment.

That phase of her activity is beyond my ken; I have enough difficulty deciphering the curious events that transpire whenever she visits. In June of 1980, she made her annual trek to Washington to give a talk and "to psychometrize the area for insight into what will happen during the coming year." As usual, she conjured up some incredible predictions (my skeptic husband chuckled at her declaration that the United States had perfected an invisible airplane until the government announcement proved her correct), none so amazing as the return of Margaret.

Let me explain.

Knowing that Jackie enjoys sightseeing, I invited her to name her pleasure, expecting her to choose a museum or a nearby plantation.

Instead, she stared at me strangely and intoned, "A spirit is asking us to go to Annapolis."

"One of my relatives made the flag, 'Don't Give Up The Ship,' that hangs at the Naval Academy," I remembered.

"Yes, I know," Jackie replied, serenely enigmatic. "I receive the name of Martha —no, I believe it's Margaret."

"Margaret it

Portrait of Margaret Forster Steuart.

is," I confirmed, casting her a surreptitious glance, quite certain that we had never discussed my illustrious relative.

We reached the U.S. Naval Academy's Visitors Center at high noon, just in time for the walking tour. It was all very pleasant, informative, and routine—until we mounted the front steps of Bancroft Hall. Jackie saw it first.

"There's your flag," she hissed.

It hung directly before us at the top of a commanding staircase rising from the main entrance hall. As the tour guide pointed to the flag and began speaking, I chimed in, "My great-great grandmother made it."

Tossing me a long, hard stare, the guide continued her discourse, " . . . and the flag was sewn by an unknown sailmaker from Erie."

"Oh, no," I protested. "The flag was made by Margaret Forster

163

Steuart, my great-great grandmother."

"That's not what the plaque says," the guide said. Her authoritative voice expressed considerable annoyance at my rudeness.

Jackie nudged me, whispering, "Margaret's here with us. I can feel her presence."

I felt only embarrassment. After all, I had interrupted the tour guide and irritated the others in our group. For the rest of the tour, I trailed quietly behind, oddly astounded by my newly surfaced feeling of camaraderie with Margaret Forster Steuart.

When I left Jackie at National Airport for her flight back to New York City, her parting words were, "Margaret wants you to help her get credit for making the flag. She made a great contribution to history and deserves to be acknowledged by the public."

Absurd, you say? So did I. And yet. . . .

The family history was in the first packing box I opened. No small miracle, because more than thirty unopened ones awaited us, thanks to our most recent move. Call it coincidence; Jackie would call it pre-ordained.

The book literally fell open to the section on Margaret's family and photocopies of a chapter in *Dr. William Egle's Notes and Queries for 1897*, written by historian Alfred Sanderson. The heading, "Perry's Flag," was subtitled, "Made by Mrs. Margaret Forster Steuart, A Native of Paxtang."

After a lengthy account of the events leading up to the Battle of Lake Erie on September 10, 1813, Sanderson narrated the following:

The flag, the emblem of Perry's victory, was made at Erie. It is about nine feet square, of close woven, coarse muslin or sheeting, in color dark blue, almost black, now rather frequently patched. The letters are of white muslin, thirteen inches wide. The dark blue of the material is now quite rusty, while the letters are yellowed with age. It is preserved in a case in the library of the United States Naval Academy at Annapolis, Maryland.

The flag, Sanderson confirmed, was made at the request of Lieutenant Oliver Hazard Perry by Margaret Forster Steuart, wife of Captain Thomas Steuart, at their home on Fourth Street near

French. Following the Battle of Erie, Perry stayed in the village as a guest of Margaret's brother, Colonel (later General) Thomas Forster, Jr. A personal friend of Perry for many years, Forster lived on French Street just around the corner from the Steuart home.

Margaret was assisted by her sister, Dorcas Bell, wife of Captain William Bell, and Mrs. Bell's daughters, Jane and Elizabeth. After the war, Jane married Samuel Hays and Elizabeth married her fiancé, James Tewksbury of the United States Navy, who was badly wounded in the Battle of Lake Erie.

The guest list that day embraced both social and patriotic purposes. To honor the friendship of her brother, Colonel Thomas Forster, Jr., with Perry, Margaret also invited Forster's daughters. Elizabeth Rachel, Mary Theodosia, and Catherine Ann were experts at domestic chores, having kept house for their father since the death four years earlier of their mother, the former Sarah Petit Montgomery. They were enthusiastic participants in the project, for their hearts were with men in the thick of the fighting. After the war, Elizabeth married James E. Herron, an artillery officer of the United States Army who had been taken prisoner by the British. Mary Theodosia married Colonel John Harris of the United States Navy, who became commandant of the Marine Corps, while Catharine Ann became the wife of Richard T. Timberlake.

The Forster girls also brought along their sisters, Hannah, eight, and Margaret, six. No matter that the youngest girls did little more than run errands, that moment in history remained fresh in their minds and when it was time to choose a life partner, both married career Army men destined to become generals. Hannah married Edward Vose Sumner, and Margaret married George Wright. As was the custom, Margaret accompanied her husband wherever his command took him. Thus, en route to a new assignment shortly after the close of the Civil War, they died together when the ship *Brother Jonathan* sank off Portland, Oregon, on July 30, 1865.

But when the young women gathered to create the flag destined to turn the tide of the war, none envisioned what the future held. They knew only of the past, a heritage that prepared them for their role in that place and time. Margaret Forster Steuart was of colonial stock, the great granddaughter of Captain Moses Dickey of the French and Indian War of 1747-48, and daughter of John fforster [sic], an officer in Provincial service during the later French and Indian War, and in the Revolution.

She was born in Paxtang, Lancaster County (now Dauphin), Pennsylvania., about two miles north of Harrisburg. The exact date of her birth eludes us, but we know she was thirty-three years old when the flag was made at her house in July 1813. As one of the foremost matrons of the little village of Erie and mother of five young children ranging in age from nine to less than one year, she must have been torn between caring for her family and doing her share for the community's war preparations. Army units were stationed nearby, while the lake harbor, barely two blocks from her home, was filled with naval vessels in various stages of construction.

Sanderson describes the Steuart home facing the lake as, . . . *a double, one-storied log and frame building . . . The room in which the flag was made . . . was cheerful, well lighted and well heated by wood in an old fashioned fireplace.* Because Erie was a young town, homes contained only the bare necessities. In the spring and summer of 1813, the citizens were grateful for their meager belongings, all the easier to load into a wagon and flee inland fifteen miles to Waterford, should the enemy arrive and occupy Erie.

As I finished reading Sanderson's account, I envisioned Margaret Forster Steuart bustling about the village of Erie during the summer of 1813 while rumors abounded at every street corner and doorway. Now, as each day dawned, she wondered if the time had come to load her belongings onto a wagon and escape. An evacuation plan devised by her husband and other village leaders seemed to be the only hope of eluding certain British invasion, but Margaret and many citizens resolutely remained in Erie.

Perhaps Margaret stood firm because self-reliance was an integral part of her heritage. Both her grandfather and father, revolutionaries in their own right, were descended from the sturdy Scotch-Irish who sailed from Ulster to the colonies early in the 18th century and settled in Paxtang. There, in 1716, they established Historic Paxton [sic] Meeting House, recognized today as the oldest Presbyterian church building in continuous use in Pennsylvania, and the second oldest in the United States.

Every inch as stalwart as her ancestors, Margaret Steuart had no intention of deserting her husband and the other military men in Erie until the settlement was clearly doomed. So it was that she was home when her brother, Colonel Thomas Forster, stopped by to introduce his close friend, Lieutenant Oliver Hazard Perry.

Margaret listened to Perry's account of the battle that earlier had taken the life of Captain James Lawrence. Moved by the dying officer's last words, she asked Perry how the women of Erie could participate and prove their patriotism.

By this time, Perry had observed her needlework skills in evidence around the room, and he made a request that astounded her: Would she construct a flag to inspire the battle-weary American sailors? Simple in design, it would bear the brave Lawrence's final plea—"Don't give up the ship!"

Swiftly enlisting the aid of her sister Dorcas and the Forster nieces, Margaret completed the flag within a few days and delivered it to Perry. He guarded the secret closely, planning to unfurl it before his men should their courage began to falter.

That moment arrived during the heat of the Battle of Lake Erie on September 10, 1813. The American sailors watched it being hoisted on the brig *Lawrence*, one of the nine vessels constructed at nearby Presque Isle.

Within minutes, their hope was renewed. After the Lawrence was disabled by cannon fire, Perry fearlessly transported the treasured flag to the ship *Niagara* in an open boat, assisted by only a few men.

Just as Margaret Steuart and Captain Perry had anticipated, this simple flag helped Perry and his men achieve an impossible victory, despite the British Navy's overwhelming strength.

If Margaret could visit Erie today, she would find the Fourth Street site of her modest home occupied by Lafayette Place, an office complex. A few blocks away, at the foot of State Street near the public dock, the rotting hulk of Perry's flagship *Niagara* was transformed over a period of several years by 20th Century artisans into the majestic tall ship that emerged victorious from the Battle of Lake Erie.

SO THERE IT WAS. If Margaret's spirit (or whatever Jackie had sensed) wanted me to prevent the story of her achievement from becoming "thin air," she succeeded masterfully. After our trip to Annapolis, I dashed off a copy of the Sanderson article to the tour guide, expecting nothing to come of it. After all, I was puncturing a naval tradition. How could one hope to replace the bronze plaque firmly ensconced on the Academy wall honoring an "unknown sailmaker"?

I underestimated the Navy's love of history. The guide I had written to, the wife of a career officer, lost no time replying that she had made copies of the information I sent her so the guides could incorporate it into their lectures.

Now I don't know if it was truly Margaret's ethereal presence that contacted Jackie. But I do know that if, as Jackie believes, Margaret made contact from the afterworld in order to receive recognition for the flag, she has prevailed with determination matching that of Captain James Lawrence, whose dying words continue to convey hope to legions on both land and sea.

On September 10, 1988, as a guest of the City of Erie along with other descendants of those present at the Battle of Lake Erie, I watched the *Niagara*, now the official flagship of the Commonwealth of Pennsylvania, slip into the waters of Lake Erie. A cool breeze hovered about my shoulder.

Some might attribute it to autumn winds ruffling the chilly waters. I am not beyond believing that it was the spirit of Margaret Forster Steuart, who never gave up the ship.

Civilians
in
Wartime

War is a malignant disease, an idiocy, a prison,
and the pain it causes is beyond telling or meaning,
but war was our condition and our history,
the place we had to live in.
— Martha Gelhorn

THE WANDERERS

by Gunter David
Fort Washington, Pennsylvania
2004

PARIS 1963

The Arc de Triomphe casts its shadows toward me, approaching the sidewalk cafe, where I've been seated for hours, it seems, at a table in the front row. I'm watching the crowds of young couples intertwined and old shoppers lugging packages.

When was it I met Georg Rosenbaum here, my friend and former brother-in-law, who came from Berlin to warn me about mortal danger only a few hundred miles away?

Georg, he isn't coming. Not this time.

BERLIN 1933

I approach my store on the Kurfurstendamm, the major thoroughfare furling through the city. Yesterday, in the Reichstag, as thousands cheered, Adolf Hitler was appointed the leader of his people.

Today, walking briskly, then almost running, I see bold writing on the showcase windows. "Jewish Swine Get Out" and "No Jews Wanted Here" and swastikas wherever there is space. In bloody red.

I want to turn away. But no! I reach for my keys and unlock the front door. I search the shop for rags, pick up a bucket, which I fill with water. I grab a ladder, and now I'm washing the glass clean, clean of the filth of my enemies.

Then I wait. The saleswomen come to work, to sell shoes made to order for ladies of the theater and films, and for wealthy women who like to mingle with the show folk. Shoes made of silk or fine leather, suede or shiny and smooth. The workmen arrive, climbing the stairs to the second floor, where they will fill past orders, working by hand.

But where are the customers? Morning turns to afternoon. We are all there, the employees and I, and then Hela, my wife, and our little Gunter holding her hand, stop in. No one else. Heads shaking, we file out at dusk.

Driving home gives me time to think about the future, whether there is one for us here in Berlin, in Germany.

"We were born here," Hela says, after putting Gunter to bed. "Your family and mine have lived here for generations. To give up everything you've worked for? Just pick up and leave?"

After a restless night of whispering and semi-sleeping, a nightmare (for me), tears for Hela, we decide to wait. Let's see what happens, we agree.

A few ladies filter in the following day. Hitler is an unspoken word. Some days later, Ursel and Lotti and Ella, ladies of the chorus, are shopping again. Marlene, the big star, drops in at the end of the week. Yet when I arrive in the morning to open the store, my heart still races.

When thousands of Nazis in brown uniforms, swastikas on their arms, goose step down the Kurfurstendamm, right past my store, their arms extended, shouting "Heil Hitler!" I feel icy cold.

We must get out of Germany, we decide. But where to?

171

"I know a place," Hela says suddenly. "Palestine. The Holy Land. The land of the Jews."

Palestine? Two thousand years have passed since the Jews lived there. "Hela," I say, "Arabs live there now, and there's not much more than sand. And what would I do in Palestine? Sell ladies shoes made to order?"

"Thousands of Jews live there now," she says. "At least we'll be among our own."

Within a week I have sold the store. And then I'm off to Palestine, "just to see what it's like," as Hela suggested. She stays behind with little Gunter, until she hears from me. I should be taking them along, my wife and little boy, on this long journey by rail and ship to another continent. Yet we have agreed that my going alone, getting a feel for the land, makes more sense. After all, I'll be back in three months.

I wave to them from the window of the train that takes me to France, on the first leg of my journey. They stand there, on the platform, waving and crying, as I do myself, deep inside of me. Now they're just dots, and then the train curves and my Hela and Gunter are out of my sight.

Tel Aviv 1933

The ship docks in Jaffa, an Arabic city, because Tel Aviv, the new Jewish one, has no port, and I climb down a rope ladder into a row boat. One Arab man helps me with this acrobatic exercise, while the other keeps the boat balanced, as other passengers follow. The luggage soon arrives at the spot where I have landed, in the land of the Jews and Arabs. Or maybe it's the land of Arabs and Jews. There are so many more of them, hundreds of thousands more Arabs than Jews.

This is what Horst, another German Jew, explains on the terrace of the Kaete Dan in Tel Aviv, a small hotel on the shore of the Mediterranean. "They don't want us here," he says, stirring sugar into his tea. "The Arabs have been living here since the seventh century, when they followed their prophet out of the Arabian Peninsula."

Somehow, I tell him, I thought that had all been settled. The British, who rule Palestine, allow the Jews into the country if they have enough money, if the applicant for the Certificate of Entry can prove to be self-supporting.

"Yes," he says. "But nobody asked the Arabs."

I travel around the small country, looking for opportunities that elude me. Tel Aviv, the Hill of Spring, is no Berlin. Ladies don't wear fancy shoes made to order. I visit a *kibbutz*, a communal settlement, where little Gunter would be raised by strangers in the Children's House and see his parents only in the afternoon. I look at the chicken coops and the cows in the pasture, and the sheep and their shepherds. It's there I would be working, with Hela on duty in the communal kitchen. Then I think of the city where I live, the hustle and bustle of cars and buses, theaters and cabarets, operas and concerts, men and women fashionably dressed, the car we bought just a year ago, and the language. How will I ever learn the language, this Hebrew?

If not shoes, and no *kibbutz*, what else could I do? How could I make a living? There's a lot of construction going on, new apartment houses. The laborers are doctors and lawyers and teachers and merchants, now in a land where they are starting anew. And then I'm there, too, in new khaki shorts and undershirt and sandals, mixing concrete, turning it into bricks, together with men from Germany, Russia, and Poland, and Lithuania, and other countries, which they left for a better future in what they call the Promised Land. During breaks they talk about how they're building a new land for their people, and what does it matter what they used to do?

Arabs on camels, their white *kefiyas* with black cords wrapped around their heads, traverse the sun-beaten sands all round us, like Arabian Nights come alive.

Alone in a furnished room I've rented after leaving the hotel, I'm getting ready for the night. Sirens in the distance are coming closer, there's banging on my door, the landlady, and she motions to the balcony. Flames are shooting into the sky, and we stand there, wordlessly, this old woman and I.

"Arabs," she says in the morning, a newspaper in her hands. "They don't want us here."

On the construction site, we stand around the charred buildings. Then, we start mixing the cement to turn it into bricks.

That evening, I write a letter to Hela. "Germany may not be the place for us," I write, "but Palestine isn't either. There'll never be peace here. I'm heading home."

A week or so later, a cable arrives from Georg. He is leaving Berlin and wants to meet me in Paris on my way home. I cable back where and when I can be reached in Paris. On the boat to Marseilles, watching the shore of the Promised Land, of this disputed sliver of land, recede in the distance, I think, *My God, what next?*

PARIS 1933

The Arc de Triomphe casts its shadows over me, approaching the sidewalk cafe of my hotel, where I've been seated at a table in the front, watching the crowds for Georg. He arrives, then, a chunky man, his red hair over his freckled forehead, smiling at me. I rise and we embrace.

Later, in my room, Georg tells me he has fled Berlin. He has learned that the Nazis have plans for the Jews. They want Germany to be only for Aryans. They want to cleanse Germany of Jews, like exterminating roaches from a house. He is stopping in Paris on his way to Holland, to warn me.

"Don't even go back to Berlin," he says, his light blue eyes looking at me intensely. "Bring Hela and little Gunter to Paris. She is ready to pack, to take all the money out of the bank, take the child and get on the train. Just call her up. And watch what you say."

We talk about his plans. Why Holland? Georg, with a doctorate in chemical engineering, has Dutch friends who will help him get settled.

"I often wonder," Georg says. "The Bible tells us we're the

'Chosen People.' Chosen for what? Persecution? Extermination?"

I have no answers.

Georg rises. His train for Amsterdam leaves in an hour. Will we ever see each other again? I take him to the station, where we relive moments from our intertwined past, as we wait for his train to arrive. I thank him for having made this special trip to Paris; he may well have saved the lives of my little family. We wish each other good luck. "And safety," George says. As he steps into the car, he turns around and shouts, *"Auf wiedersehen!"*

Some weeks later, I'm at the train station once more, and there they are, my beloved Hela and Gunter, stepping off the train from Berlin to the platform, where I stand, waving to them, then hugging and kissing them, taking the suitcases from the porter.

PARIS 1963

Hela joins me at the table on the sidewalk. Back in 1935, when our French visa expired after two years, we chose moving to Palestine after all. Returning to Paris had been Hela's idea. Visiting the hotel, walking on the Champs-Elysees, driving out to St. Cloud. "Remember when we lived on that second floor, in those rooms in the farmhouse. It had no kitchen, and I cooked on the toilet seat cover?"

"So when you cooked, we couldn't go to the bathroom." I nod, smiling. It wasn't funny then, I say, remembering how I sold shoes door-to-door, until the French said, *voila*, time is up.

Gunter is no longer little, but married with children, living in America. We, in our retirement, are revisiting the past. After Paris comes Berlin.

Today, at our little round table, Hela and I tell each other how we wished Georg could be here with us, at this cafe, to which he once came to save our lives. We recall a day in May, 1940, when we and some friends were clustered around the short-wave radio in our apartment in Tel Aviv. We heard the guttural sounds of the announcer reporting from Radio Berlin that the march of his

Fuehrer's troops into Holland had begun. Georg, who had sought a haven in Holland, soon would be wearing a yellow Star of David, to proclaim his identity, his vulnerability, as he walked the streets of Amsterdam.

Yes, what about Georg?

We shall visit him too. At the memorial in Bergen Belsen.*

REFERENCES

* *The Holocaust Martyrs' and Heroes' Remembrance Authority*, *www.yadvashem.org*

FAMILY GIFTS

by Helen Dorothy Kuehn Gamelin
Pacific Palisades, California
2001

Hildegard must have been watching from the window, because there she is, standing on the sidewalk smiling tentatively, looking exactly like the photo she sent my sister and me last September.[1]

Berlin! It's three p.m., a week before Easter, 2001, and snowflakes drift from a leaden sky.[2] The cars and trucks roaring down the boulevard have begun to turn on their headlights.

Now Phyllis and I, shivering in our California cottons, shake hands with Hildegard, and follow her quickly up the stairs. We are second cousins, meeting for the first time, and Hildegard has invited us to celebrate her seventieth birthday.[3]

We've only had time to exchange a few letters and photos with Hildegard since we "found" her last July—after more than eleven years of searching.[4] In one of the scans Phyllis sent her, Hildegard recognized the confirmation photo of her grandmother, Martha, taken in turn-of-the-century Berlin.[5] By that time, Martha's brother Joseph Kuehn, our grandfather, had finished his apprenticeship and left Berlin forever.[6] When Joseph died in California fifty years later, our families lost contact.[7] We've brought a dozen dog-eared unidentified photos from Joseph's desk. If only Hildegard can bring them to life with names, dates, and memories!

It's warm in the living room, the *Stube*. Here's the fringed silk curtain we've seen in Hildegard's snapshots, and beyond, a fir tree and apartments. Cacti and succulents crowd the windowsills. A cut-glass ashtray cradles an Iron Cross and the hideous bullet that nearly killed Hildegard's father at Verdun. The coffee table is spread with pretzels and chocolates. Hildegard has opened her home to us, virtual strangers.

Hildegard eases her swollen feet out of her slippers, and for a moment, we just look at each other—three middle-aged women, all mothers of young adult children. Hildegard is a few years older, but a lifetime of hard work and poor health has aged her. She is still mourning the death of her beloved husband.[8] The pain and loneliness of her letters dismayed us. She urges us to switch to the familiar *du* form, which makes us uneasy.

Now we're sipping raspberry tea and Hildegard is speaking quickly, in German. Amazingly, we understand her! Without knowing it, we've spent years preparing for this visit: Phyllis studied German in high school and, on retirement, I took every German class at our community college.[9] As an exchange student with a German family, Phyllis became sensitive to household customs and manners. She tells me, for example, that inside doors, even the bathroom door, are usually kept closed.[10]

We pull out presents: dried fruit and nuts from the San Joaquin Valley, a coffee table book on California, an Angels' jersey and cap for Hildegard's son, Erik. We set our very best present on the table before her. The photo album bound in blue cloth contains everything we know about the family so far—scans of old photos, family trees, snapshots of our parents, children, grandchildren, and our houses. There's a big packet of blank pages for new photos—Phyllis wants names, dates, facts, while I want to walk the gas-lit streets of our grandfather's Berlin.

On the cover of the album is a blow-up of our common ancestor, our great-grandmother, a young Polish-German widow with two small children, Joseph and Martha. Stamped by a Berlin photo studio, the portrait[11] was taken in the 1880s, shortly after they arrived in the city. Six-year-old Joseph (our grandfather) wears shiny tasseled boots, clearly supplied by the studio. He stares into the camera, his shoulders squared, looking frightened. Hildegard's grandmother, Martha, an enchantingly lovely four-year-old in an elaborate dress, rests her hand in her mother's lap.

But Hildegard barely glances at the album.

We are anxious to learn more about Martha, the hard-working, long-suffering mother of our family legends. But, an hour later, Hildegard is deep in the story of an ungrateful neighbor and the album still sits unopened on the coffee table. She even spills water on it from a vase of crocuses as she reaches for the ringing phone.

"*Ja-ja*," we hear. "*Alles in Ordnung.*"[12]

We stagger upstairs for a nap. "What did we do wrong?" I ask Phyllis. "Why doesn't she like the album?"

Phyllis shrugs.

"I bet that was Erik on the phone," she says, "checking if he should dump us back at the airport."

We fall into a troubled sleep.

When we wake up, Hildegard calls us to sit beside her. The album lies in her lap, and she is looking at photos of our children, trying to pronounce their names.

As Hildegard talks, the fog gradually clears. Her father's relatives, not ours, had time and love to give her as a child. Her grandmother, Martha, the little girl on the album, grew into a spiteful old lady, pitting her daughters against each other. Martha outlived them all. When Hildegard's mother died, she called Oma Martha. "So, the _____ is dead,"[13] Martha rasped, before Hildegard hung up on her forever.

We are appalled.

Hildegard vaguely remembers a call reporting Martha's death, but knows nothing more. From us she heard her great-grandmother's name for the first time. There are no cousins or nephews to interview. Hildegard is alone in her generation, as is Erik in his. She confesses that Phyllis ("Philip" to her) bears an eerie resemblance to Martha. She looks up at Phyllis impishly. "Are you Martha, come back to haunt me?"

We try to be patient as Hildegard, stony-faced, drones on about "friends" who dropped her after her husband's death. Connivers are after her money. Nobody visits and nobody listens. Even happy stories of her marriage, and Erik's childhood, are tinged with sorrow.

This house is a shadowy prison. Hildegard seems to want only our pity.

Imperceptibly, the war becomes the elephant in the room. Hildegard was born in 1931, two years before Hitler took power. We know nothing of her wartime experiences. Curious as we are, we wouldn't dream of asking her to revisit those memories.

We sink into the sofa, stuffed with Mexican food from Hildegard's favorite restaurant. Now Phyllis pulls "baby pictures" out of her purse. Her chickens!

"They give me lots of eggies," Phyllis says fondly.[14]

"And baby chicks?" Hildegard asks.

"Oh, no," says Phyllis, deadpan. "They haven't figured that out yet." Hildegard's mouth twists. A few minutes later, she rushes into the kitchen. We hear her repeat something out loud, followed by a torrent of laughter. She comes out, wiping her eyes.

"That's the first time I've laughed in six years," she says. "Since my husband died."[15]

I've hung up the dishtowel and Phyllis—*Liebe* Phyllis now—is making tea. Hildegard—Hilde now—sits at the kitchen table, shoes off, contemplating faded photos.

"Now I see why Martha was so mean," Hilde says.[16] "I was so young when she died. Martha's only four in this photo ... and they lived on the streets. They were *Moritaeten* singers.[17] Listen, this is all I have from Martha ..."

To our surprise, Hilde begins to sing:

Mutter, Mutter, hin ist hin!
Verloren ist verloren ...

Mother, Mother, what's done is done!
What's lost is lost forever ...[18]

Hilde gets a faraway look. "What I really wish I had," she continues, stacking the photos, "is Fitzi's diary."

The Great Depression. Fitzi, her Uncle Fritz, took care of little Hilde while her parents worked long hours at their fruit and vegetable stand in the central market. Fritz had been unemployed for five years when Hitler rescued him with a factory job. Fritz immediately joined the Nazi Party. By that time, Hilde's parents had opened their store. They had no time for politics.

"*Na, ja,*" she continues, "when we turned ten, we girls went to BdM (*Bund deutscher Maedel*, the League of German Girls, the girl's counterpart of Hitler Young).[19] Our uniform was a blue skirt and white blouse. Twice a week, we sewed things for the soldiers, played games, sang *Hitlerlieder*. But my career in the BdM didn't last long.

"Each morning, my mother tied my braids with hair ribbons to match my dress." She smoothes her jet-black hair, wispy now from chemotherapy. "I had such thick hair then," she says wistfully.

"One day, our BdM leader, a young man, ripped off my hair ribbons and berated me in front of my classmates for wearing 'finery,' which our Fuhrer forbade. My hair flew all over the place, and I was in tears. Mother was furious, and she never let me set foot in another BdM meeting.

"Well, the next week, the BdM leader showed up at our store. Mother kept him waiting a while before she lit into him:

" 'I'm terribly sorry! *Tut mir furchtbar Leid!* ' " Hilde bellows, stabbing the air with her finger. " 'My daughter was perfectly correct! I could understand it if the ribbons were plaid or orange, but they're blue, they match her uniform perfectly, and they're necessary!

Now, if you'll excuse me, I have work to do!' Then she slammed the storeroom door."

Hilde chuckles at her mother's courage.

It's getting dark. Wooden roller blinds rumble down on schedule, first in the *Stube*, now in the kitchen, and we turn on the light. They are part of Hilde's security system, but she's far away now, in wartime Berlin where they cannot protect her.

"After school, I helped in the store. Mother stamped the ration cards, showing what each person bought. Jews had to shop Friday afternoons, after everyone else. They got the 'hunger card,' but Mother figured out how to give them a little more. She kept a piece of blank paper on the counter, and stamped that instead of their ration cards, urging them to come earlier next week. She could have been denounced!

"One day—I was eleven—my mother pushed me into the *Stube* and shut the door. I peeked through the curtain and saw a truck stop in front of my friend's apartment building. Four Gestapo jumped out. Leah and her mother came out on the sidewalk and climbed into the truck. Her father was a doctor, old, an educated man, *ne*? He walked slowly, so the Gestapo kicked him into the truck and then sped away. I never saw Leah again ..."

Hilde's blue eyes fill with tears. Phyllis puts her arm around her. Hilde coughs and hurries on.

"Neighbor boys, heading for the Eastern Front, came to say goodbye. Each time the door closed behind one, Mother would say, 'We won't be seeing him again.' And she was right. But to say so was treason in the Hitler time—defeatism. All the boys I grew up with are gone. My cousin Willi—he was four years older—he was only eighteen years old when the letter came: missing in action at Stalingrad.[20] ... Sometimes I imagine he survived and is living in Siberia with a wife and children."

A long pause. The candle is guttering under the teapot.

"We slept in the cellar," she almost whispers. "We listened to the BBC, which was illegal, and when they announced an air raid, we knew we had about two hours. All our windows got blown out, even the windows of my dollhouse—they were real glass and went up and down. My father covered the big windows with newspaper, so I did the same for the dollhouse windows. My dolls were bombed out!

"When they stopped bombing our neighborhood, we'd go up on the roof and watch the waves of bombers pass overhead. Berlin was silent and pitch black, with now and then a flash of blue light from the tram lines. The bombs made a terrible noise—*sssssseeeeeeeek.* The horizon got bright as day.

"Once an incendiary bomb fell through the roof and landed in a wicker chair. My father ran upstairs and threw the whole thing out onto the street, where it broke into hundreds of flaming fragments. It was laundry day. Wet sheets hanging up there probably saved our building. My father got a medal and became an air-raid warden.

"Bombed-out families lived in our school. There were no more classes. Then we children were evacuated to Bad Warmbrunn.[21] The Russian Army drove us back to Berlin. People lived in ruins. My parents moved into our storeroom, and I slept on the floor by their bed.

"Papers came ordering my father to report to the Front, although he was an old man whose hand shook when he ate. The streets were barricaded with sofas and burnt-out trams. The *Volkssturm* sent boys my age and old men to fight to death as Russian tanks bore down on them.[22]

"Well, Mother already had a scheme to save my father. She had donated blood throughout the war, and now her friends at the hospital admitted her as a patient. The store was 'essential.' Without Mother to keep it running, my father couldn't go to the Front.

"War is horrible!" Hilde continues. "The Russians wanted revenge. Soldiers stomped into the store, stole my father's watch and a few jars of Mother's jam and smashed the rest. For days, Mother and I hid under a pile of cabbages with sacks over our heads. Drunken soldiers said, '*Frau komm!*' Every night we heard screams—little girls even.

"We had nothing in the store. My father suggested standing my dolls in the window to cheer up passers-by. An American came in, asking to buy them. My Tini and Gretel emigrated!" Hilde laughs.

The war ended. Hilde's aging parents had little energy for the store. Cigarettes replaced money on the Black Market. Joseph sent them regular packages, which were converted to cigarettes on the Black Market, then to food.[23]

"I got so sick of my one dress," Hilde says.

When her mother's health failed, Hilde quit school and took her place behind the counter. At night school, she because a licensed pedicurist and self-supporting. In 1961, as the Berlin Wall went up, she married. She was thirty. Her parents now spent all their time and money on Lotto. Hilde's mother took her own life in 1964, and her father committed suicide a few years later.

"After the *Wende*," Hilda concludes, "I reclaimed our old apartment in East Berlin, and sold it to buy this house.[24] My husband only had four years in it."

Silence. It's midnight, and Hilde pinches out the candle. We are drained, exhausted by the futility of Hitler's Reich. We go up to bed without speaking, having forgotten to eat *Abendbrod*, the evening meal.

OUR WEEK IN BERLIN has become a cherished memory. The faded photos remain unidentified, but we have come home with wonderful gifts: We have new insight into our Kuehn ancestors. The savage industrial slums of Berlin shaped Joseph and his sister, Martha. That legacy echoes through both our families.

What's more, Hilde is writing her memoirs! "I understand many things better now," she says.[25] She really enjoys writing. *"Es macht mir sehf viel Spass!"* Hilde has already outlined chapters and dates, beginning in her childhood.

The memoir ends, our new relative tells us, "when you find me."[26]

REFERENCES

1. For this article, the writer has changed our cousin's name to protect her privacy. Hildegard was her mother's name. Her son's name has been similarly changed. The writer would like to thank Edelgard Kirchoff Ditmars for insights into cultural aspects of World War II.

2. Helen Gamelin, *Journals* (Los Angeles, CA., n. published, 2001). n. page.

3. *Hildegard to Phyllis Kuehn and Helen Gamelin,* 2 Nov. 2000, Berlin. Original in possession of Phyllis Kuehn. Hildegard states her birth date is 19 April, 1931. Hitler's birthday was 20 April.

4. The process of finding Hildegard has been documented by the writer, but lies outside the scope of this article.

5. Original owned by Phyllis Kuehn.

6. *Marriage Certificate* for Joseph Kuehn and Emilie Rauhut, 9 July, 1898, Oxx., The Netherlands, provincie Noord-Brabant, #51, original owned by Phyllis Kuehn.

7. Ibid.

8. *Hildegard to Phyllis Kuehn and Helen Gamelin,* 10 Aug., 2000, Berlin. Hildegard's husband: 6.8.1927-18.9.1997.

9. *Oral Interview With Phyllis Kuehn,* 28 Sept. 2001, by the writer.

10. Phyllis lived with a German family in Lengerich, Nordrhein, Wesrfalen.

11. Original owned by Phyllis Kuehn.

12. Oral interview with Hildegard 7 April, 2001, Berlin, by writer, recorded in writer's *Journals.* "Yes, yes. Everything's OK." The writer's translation.

13. Oral Interview With Hildegard, 8 April 2001, Berlin, by writer, recorded in writer's *Journals.* The writer did not translate the vulgar word Martha used in relation to the death of her own daughter. The German is as follows: "Also, Das Aas ist tot." Hildegard believes that Martha died around 1966.

14. Oral Interview With Hildegard and Phyllis Kuehn, 9-10 April, 2001, Berlin, by the writer, recorded in the writer's *Journals.*

15. Hildegard to Phyllis Kuehn and Helen Gamelin, 10 August, 2000.

16. Oral interview with Hildegard and Phyllis Kuehn, 12 April, 2001, Berlin, by the writer, recorded in the writer's *Journals.*

17. Erwin Sternktzke, *Der Stilisierte Bankelsang* (Marburg: Dissertationsdruckerei und Verlag Konrad Triltsch, 1933), pp. 3-89 [URL PT 581 B3S8] updated from Internet: www.ib.hu-berline.de/~wumsta

/rehn5.html.

"The Moritaetensinger (or Baenkelsinger) represents a German tradition that possibly started in Augsburg around 1508, at the time printed newspapers first appeared. Sometimes called the 'poor man's opera,' the singer stood on a bench (Bank) or in the marketplace and sang of Moritaten (crimes or disasters) while pointing to a sequence of illustrations with a stick. The main point was the moral: Crime doesn't pay and the criminal will be punished. In 1928, during a period of cultural flowering in Berlin, Kurt Weill (1900-1950) and Bertolt Brecht (1898-1956) based their opera Die Dreigroschenoper (The Threepenny Opera) on the haunting, melancholy ballads of the Moritaetensinger. Americans are familiar with the song, Mack the Knife, from The Threepenny Opera. In 1981, the Munich Stadtmuseum held an exhibition of Moritaeten songs and art. The last-known Moritaeten artist was Adam Holbin (1855-1921) of Holstein. Ernst Becker sang and recorded Moritaetenlieder in the 1960s."

18. Translation by the writer.

19. Alison Owings, Frauen: German Women Recall the Third Reich (New Brunswick, NY, Rutgers University Press, 1993), p. 477. [SM 943 086] The BdM (Bund deutscher Maedel) often written in English as BDM, was the League of German Girls, the girls' counterpart of Hitler Young (Hitler Jugend). These organizations were more or less mandatory because their aim was to indoctrinate Aryan German children with Nazi propaganda. Hildegard was briefly in the Jungmaedel (Young Girls), the division of the BdM for girls from ten to fourteen years old.

20. The Encyclopaedia Britannica Inc. The New Encyclopedia Britannica, vol. 19 (15th ed.; Chicago: William Benton, publisher, 1974), pp. 993-994. The Battle of Stalingrad (summer 1942-2 Feb, 1943) was the turning point in the war for Hitler. The fall of Stalingrad marked the end of the German advance in Russia, and the beginning of the Soviet counteroffensive. The RAF and U.S. Army Air Force began bombing Berlin heavily in early 1943.

21. Bibliographisches Institut, Meyers Enzykopaedisches Lexicon, Baud 3 (Manaheim: Lexikonverlag, 1971), p. 364.

22. Alexandra Richie, Faust's Metropolis, A History of Berlin, (New York: Carroll & Graf Publishers Inc., 1998) pp. 583-584.

23. Affidavit of Martha Schwarz, nee Kuhn, Translation. Executed in Berlin, 4 Nov. 1954, Dr. Fritz Kayser, Notary Public, 30 Neue Beyreuther Str., Berlin W. No. 147 of the Notary Public's Records, The Estate of Joseph Kuehn, Bert BN. Snyder, Attorney at Law, Santa Cruz, California.

Original in possession of Phyllis Kuehn. As part of her affidavit, Martha presents a series of letters from her brother, Joseph Kuehn, listing the contents of twenty-one packages he sent her and her daughters between 23 March, 1947, and 9 March, 1948. Joseph died on 20 April, 1948, bequeathing his sister Martha $35 (U.S.) a month for as long as she lived. This was equivalent to more than 50 RM, a worker's monthly wage, and was desperately needed by Martha and her daughters in the aftermath of the war. Martha, however, had turned over all her personal documents to a dishonest notary, who was trying to get her inheritance for himself. Martha had a hard time proving her identity. Jutrocin, where Martha was born, was now in the People's Republic of Poland. Finally, the German government gave Martha new identification papers, but then sent the lot to San Jose, Costa Rica, instead of San Jose, California, where a trial was in progress—Joseph's daughter was suing to break his will. Martha did finally get her money. The funds Joseph had set aside for her ran out in 1960, by which time the value of her monthly payments was much less. In 1989, Phyllis Kuehn located Bert Snyder Jr., an attorney in Santa Cruz, who sent her his father's complete files on Joseph Kuehn's estates. The names and addresses in the Affidavits of Martha and one of her daughters provided us with a beginning in trying to find our relatives in Berlin.

24. "Die Wende," or "turning point," is how German refer to all the changes, beginning with the fall of the Berlin Wall in November 1989, and culminating with the reunification of the city of Berlin and the two Germanies, East and West.

25. Hildegard to Phyllis Kuehn and Helen Gamelin, 14 Sept. 2001, Berlin. Original in possession of the writer.

26. Hildegard to Phyllis Kuehn and Helen Gamelin, 14 Sept. 2001, Berlin. p. 3 ". . . ich werde da enden, wo Ihr mich gefunden habt."

I Saw London Burning

by Rita Berman
Chapel Hill, North Carolina
2004

I was seven years old and living in London in 1939 when
England declared war on Germany because of the invasion of
Poland. The first time I heard the wail of an air-raid siren, my
mother rushed us out of the house to take cover at the nearest public shelter. In the confusion, she had picked up my brother, the middle child, and was carrying him in her arms; while my baby sister and
I struggled to keep up. That warning siren turned out to be a practice drill. After the quiet period of what was called "The Phony
War," Germany's planes did fly overhead and drop incendiary
bombs in their attempt to destroy London. Eventually, I became
used to the wail of the sirens and the booming sound of the anti-
aircraft guns, which, to me, sounded a bit like thunder.

For months everyone had been on edge. Even though we were
separated from Europe by some thirty miles of ocean, our country
was preparing for the worst. Men were recruited for Armed Forces
or the Home Guard and their jobs were filled by women. Many took
on non-traditional work on the buses, in factories, or on farms in

what was called The Land Army. An aunt of mine was sent to work in a munitions factory, and because she was very short, under five feet, she was given a make-shift platform to stand on while she operated her machine.

When war was declared my father was one of those who joined the Home Guard, but he kept his day job in the family business. At night, after the sirens went off, he went to his assigned post where he watched for incoming German planes, noting the locations where the bombs fell so that he could pass on this information to the fire and police authorities. He also ensured that no one violated the blackout rules. All windows had to be covered with heavy, dark curtains so that no light was visible outside. The street lights were turned off, as well as lights in shop windows, to make it more difficult for enemy planes to identify London and other strategic areas.

People got used to getting up and dressing in the dark. One night, when the siren went off after we were all in bed, my father dressed in a hurry, grabbed what he thought was his underwear from the chair by the bed, and left the house.

In the morning when my mother got dressed, she couldn't find her underwear, but my father's shorts were on the chair. She grumbled at having to get out a clean pair of knickers.

In the evening when my father returned home, my mother asked, "Lew, do you know what happened to my knickers? I couldn't find them this morning, only your underwear."

He laughed. "Yes, I picked them up in the dark, and didn't know it until I went to do a wee and there was no opening in the front so I had to drop my pants."

This humorous situation arose because in those days we did not bathe or change our underwear every day. The weekly wash was done in the bath tub, using hot water produced by a gas geyser. Soiled clothes were put into the bath for my mother to wash later, kneeling and rubbing the articles on a washboard, a flat piece of wood with metal ridges, to loosen the dirt. Once a week all three of us children were put in the bathtub together.

To help protect the populace, the government offered two types of air-raid shelters; the Anderson shelter designed for erecting outside in the garden, and the Morrison shelter, a rectangular metal contraption which some of our friends installed in their dining room and used as a table. Sitting under the Morrison gave some protection from furniture and debris in the event the house was hit.

When war began, my grandparents, uncles, and an aunt on my mother's side lived next door to us. This grandfather was a blacksmith who owned a garage and forge where he made iron gates, railings, and tools, and shod horses and repaired cars. All of my uncles worked in the garage and I remember noticing that they had dirty fingernails and rough, red-looking hands.

Grandfather built a door in the fence that separated our back gardens to allow easy access between both houses. It was decided we would accept the Anderson type shelter and install it in his garden for both our families to use.

I was still of an age to play with dolls and other toys. One of my favorites was the doll house that my mother had made for me out of a used orange crate. By standing it on one end it had two rooms. Mother covered the interior walls with wallpaper and glued linoleum tile on the floors. On the outside, she had nailed some wire and made curtains that hung from this. The furniture was also handmade from scraps of wood and empty matchboxes. A wooden cotton reel with a piece of cardboard on top became a table. Small dolls were made out of pipe cleaners decorated with fabric and cotton wool. Pieces of fringed felt were turned into rugs. All very simply done, but I loved it.

I saw my uncles dig a large hole in the garden for the air-raid shelter. The metal shelter sections were bolted together. It had a roof curved like an arch. After placing the shelter into the hole, which must have been about four or five feet below the surface, my uncles covered the roof and sides with packed earth. To stabilize the building they put the earth into all sorts of containers and—they took my doll house.

To the grownups it may have been only a wooden crate, something that would hold the earth, and give more protection. But to me it was my pretty dollhouse. I didn't understand at the time, nor could I do anything about it—the grownups just took it away. I was very upset when this happened.

The finished shelter was a simple structure, furnished with four narrow bunks, smaller than single-bed size. We sat in the dark or used a flashlight. We had no heat, or air-conditioning, not even a door, just a wooden shield that was placed in front of the entrance after everyone came in.

Sometimes eight of us squeezed in, children on the top bunks and adults crouched on the bottom bunks. Eventually the night hours would pass and after hearing the all-clear siren, we emerged to face the day and whatever destruction that had taken place from the bombs and the fires.

My father's parents lived a few miles away in a large house in the E.1 borough. From here they operated the family business of "cut-make-and-trim" and made ladies' coats. This grandfather had soft, clean-looking hands. He sat at a pedal-operated Singer sewing machine sewing the garment pieces together. Several of my aunts did the hand sewing and finishing of button-holes and loops. The husband of one of my aunts pressed (ironed) the finished garments.

My father was a crucial member of this business, for he was skilled as a cutter, and designed and graded patterns into different sizes. He would place rolls of cloth out flat in layers and with a very long knife cut out the various parts of the coats.

Several years into the war, a direct hit from a bomb destroyed the house, furniture, clothes, and factory equipment. Fortunately, no one was at home, but it was a terrible shock, for now they were homeless. One of the few items found in the rubble was my father's good conduct medal that he had received when he was about eight years old. I am now the keeper of that medal. It is called "The King's Medal," is dated 1913-1914 and was presented to him for "attendance, conduct, and industry." He had not missed one single day at school for a whole year.

After their house was destroyed, my grandparents moved into a two-story flat in Brick Lane, E.1, and found new premises for the factory close to the small shops that sold trimmings, buttons, and fabrics.

Brick Lane is familiar to many American TV viewers as the site of a television show, but to me it is where my grandparents lived in a flat next door to a movie theater. A long flight of uncarpeted stairs led up to the kitchen, dining, and living rooms. Up another flight and there were three bedrooms and the bathroom. From the back door of the kitchen you could step out onto a small balcony area; here my grandmother raised chickens. One of them became like a pet and used to follow her around in the kitchen.

The East End of London suffered much damage as the war progressed. Buildings, shops, houses, even churches such as the famous St. Paul's Cathedral, were blown up or caught fire. Many people died during this time. The King and Queen, who stayed in London all during the Blitz, toured the East End and saw for themselves the devastation wrought by the German planes.

Piles of rubble from collapsed houses, broken windows or blocks of flats with exterior walls completely blown away revealing interior rooms exposed to all the elements, became a common sight. Some areas were not accessible because of unexploded bombs. Once, when walking from the train station to visit my grandparents in Brick Lane, I turned a corner and came upon a large building in flames and a group of firemen trying to put out the fire. The walls began to fall and a policeman told the watching crowd to stand back.

However, in spite of the destruction and deprivations, the population behaved stoically, maybe grumbled a bit but there were no noisy protests. I saw hand-written signs in the windows of the shopkeepers stating "Business as Usual." Everyone put up a brave front in spite of the danger.

The war continued for years, and my father was conscripted into the Army. He was issued with a uniform and assigned to the Royal Corps of Signals. Designated to be a truck driver, he didn't know how to drive but was sent to the motor pool where another serviceman explained how to crank the engine and shift gears. My father then drove three times around the motor pool, a special circular course and became a qualified driver. That was the story he told us when he came home on leave. With practice, he began more adept and learned to drive on unlit streets in unfamiliar territory.

Food was rationed and so was clothing. Each individual was issued a ration book to be marked with indelible ink after the week's rations were purchased. Each person was allowed one egg, eight ounces of butter, eight ounces of meat, and eight ounces of sugar per week. In those days, the population was thin but, we were told, quite healthy because our diet was low in calories; there was a lot of emphasis on eating vegetables and fruit, such as apples and pears which were grown in England. Those who lived in the country and raised chickens or rabbits were better off because they had something to barter.

Sometime after 1941, we were issued with powdered eggs from the United States. My mother used the egg powder to make cakes, or by adding water, made scrambled eggs.

Clothes rationing affected several of my aunts who got married during war-time: They all wore the same wedding dress made out of parachute silk.

My father was transferred to the north of England and later his unit returned to the south. He was, however, no longer driving a truck—he had found his niche as Regimental Tailor, altering the uniforms of the officers on a treadle Singer sewing machine. He also sewed on stripes and buttons.

After the Americans joined in the fight there was renewed optimism in England that the war would soon be over. We had to wait until May 1945 for the victory celebrations and our family went up to London to join in on that happy occasion.

COFFEE, DONUTS, AND STAMINA: CLUBMOBILING IN WORLD WAR II

by Tara McClellan McAndrew
Springfield, Illinois
2004

'Since I last wrote you we have moved. It was very sudden and occurred December 23," read the wartime letter. "You should have seen the smiles on the civilians' faces, they thought we were retreating."[1]

Clarice Hickox couldn't tell her parents where she had moved in her December 29, 1944, letter. She was working for the American Red Cross in Europe during World War II and following the front as a "clubmobiler," women who drove vehicles loaded with coffee, donuts, cigarettes, and American newspapers and magazines for the soldiers. Clubmobilers also greeted arriving and departing troops.

In 2004, the Springfield, Illinois, American Red Cross chapter inherited one-hundred-eighty letters and wartime memorabilia from Hickox, who had died at the age of eighty-six. The letters, written to family and friends, detail her experiences training and working for the Red Cross during the war.

Although clubmobilers were like wartime hostesses, their work

194

could be dangerous, according to Monica Mazzaro, an AmeriCorps volunteer who is inventorying Hickox's materials. "The clubmobiles were sometimes targets, because the enemy saw the Red Cross volunteers as having much-needed medical supplies," she says. Hickox went through gas chamber training so she could recognize the smell of dangerous gasses and know how to protect herself.[2]

Hickox started working for the Red Cross on April 5, 1943, shortly after graduating from Mills College. The next six months she trained on the East Coast while waiting for an assignment overseas.

In a July 2 letter from New York City that year, she wrote, "Every day I see New York casualty lists and wonder about the ones from Springfield."[3] She added that a friend "kept asking about a psychiatress [sic] and was sure we needed one" because of the uncertainty about where they were going and when. "There was one in Washington whom we were invited to call on if we wished, but I had no reason to see her."[4]

She told about packing boxes of supplies for Allied prisoners of war. "Packing those boxes yesterday nearly finished me off. I lifted three tons," Hickox wrote. She recommended that Red Cross chapters display a P.O.W. box so families could see what their boys received.[5]

"The lady in charge showed us three cards which she had just received from Allied prisoners who received the box, a card goes in each box for the prisoner to sign and send back so that Red Cross knows the boxes are received. The Swiss do all of the work of sending them and checking on their receipt," she wrote.[6]

Some of her training was "depressing," Hickox said. In a July 11, 1943 letter from New York, Hickox told about doing "case work" in Queens. Part of her job was confirming if a soldier was needed because of a family member's illness. "I just phone the doctors and hospitals to verify the stories," she wrote. "Yesterday, I had a WAC (Women's Army Corps) case where the husband claimed dependence and was having a nervous breakdown. . . ."[7]

Sometimes she was like a "private detective," Hickox added. "(We try) to locate lost sons for fathers in Veterans Hospitals, etc.

But what gets me is these frantic neurotic women who write in because they haven't heard from (their) son for five or six weeks and get themselves in a nervous state over it. They would be notified immediately by the government if he were injured, missing, or killed. On these cases it takes at least a month to get a report from the adjunct general and necessitates no end of correspondence. Then when you finally get the word to them they have already heard from the soldier."[8]

Even though she wasn't deployed yet, Hickox established a code with her parents so they could determine her future locations. "Watch the initials on (the) envelope address, Mr. H.L. Hickox (her father's name was H.V. Hickox) might begin to spell out London, or if 'Of course' appears in the tenth line, check first letter in second paragraph. Expect to use cities on map I sent home. However, we may censor our own mail or I might not feel like revealing exact spot for other reasons."[9]

Training was long, hard work. On September 18, Hickox wrote from her new post in Virginia. "We work ten hours a day, seven days a week."

Finally, she was shipped overseas in October 1943. We now know she arrived in Southampton, England, went to Ouittiot, France, traveled west to Bitburg, Germany, and traveled through Germany, ending in Regensburg, according to her framed map.[11]

Once overseas, Hickox described life there for her family. "(A friend) gave me names of several French people (in the hopes) I'll be able to look them up," she wrote on October 29. "There is no provision for writing to a French person as our Army won't accept letters and we cannot use the French post, which isn't operating any way. However, the French post operates locally, like within a city. I could write to someone in Paris and give it to someone going to Paris who would mail it there. This is what the French people do. However, this is against regulations. In a way it seems like we ought to do some of these things as it is one of (the) Red Cross functions. Especially when for four years people haven't heard from their friends and relatives outside France."[12]

After Christmas, Hickox happily wrote her mother about the numerous packages she had received from home. Always welcome were sweets and stockings, since the clubmobilers had to wear the latter and wore them out quickly. "The little Christmas tree is so cute on the desk in our room with the little things tied on: gum, inhaler, razor blades and hairpins," she wrote.[13]

Housing was often haphazard at best. "We now have a swell set up in a large city," Hickox continued. "We have a house which was hastily left and contains furniture, etc. Four of us share a nice room." But the biggest treat was spending the night at a Luxembourg hotel after Christmas. "I had a bath in a bathtub that worked and had hot water . . . I haven't been in a tub since the first of October, but we have gotten showers."[14]

Four months after arriving overseas, Hickox wrote the national American Red Cross about her work there. While the clubmobiles' donuts and coffee were popular with soldiers, their best commodity was "a perfect stream of American lingo," she wrote. "One thirty-nine-year-old sergeant told me he cried the first night after the club-mobile visited his camp. All afternoon he had stood around the clubmobile and just listened to the girls talk."[15]

"Mother was worried about our military set back of last month, but it was not on my army nor my corps, although we came to the rescue," Hickox wrote her dad January 13, 1945. She was probably referring to the Battle of the Bulge, the Germans' counterattack in Belgium December 16, 1944.[16]

"Don't worry about us, as in a retreat the clubmobiles go first," she continued in her January 13 letter. "No personnel was lost in the German breakthrough. . . . One clubmobile girl is dead but she was in a hospital for illness and it was hit by a V bomb which only broke her wrist but she died of shock."[17]

But there were light moments, too. "A few days ago we served some engineer who had loads of Schnapps and gave us a bottle. The next day we served a group of Tank Destroyers, who were living on the ground in the snow with no cover, no heat, no nothing. They asked us in a joke if we had any Schnapps so just before we left we gave them the bottle. I suppose Washington would have fits if they knew clubmobiles over here dispensed such as Schnapps, but it was not the first time and will not be the last time."[19]

Hickox wanted to publish articles about her wartime work and on April 28, 1945, she sent her parents one of her unpublished articles. "There were three of us in the cab of our clubmobile, built on a six by six truck," she wrote. "It was crowded as we all wore many clothes and also had blankets wrapped about us. When one moved, we all moved; when one smoked, we all smoked. It was better to lean forward as then your back didn't pound the back of the seat continually . . ."[20]

"You don't talk as much as you did in the family automobile because you are too tired and you have to scream to be heard. Sometimes you all sing and that is good because you feel much warmer. . . . Home! How remote, it's been almost two years. . . ."[21]

The stress of constantly moving and working added up. On March 5, 1945, Hickox wrote that she went to the hospital. "There really isn't anything wrong with me. I think I'm just worn out." Some R&R in the French Riviera helped. "Despite the fact the beaches and waters had not been cleared of mines, everyone was on them and a few swam, including me. . . . You could watch them farther out exploding mines."[22]

In Lorraine, France, the war's destruction was everywhere. "We passed fields of dead animals—sheep, horses, cattle. I guess the thrifty people butchered most of the stuff."[23]

In spring 1945, came the first hint of the war's end in Europe. "Col. Wolf quoted the radio London as saying the Germans had offered unconditional surrender," Hickox wrote on April 28. "I have been carrying a Verry pistol and four white flares to celebrate with."[24]

On May 7, Germany surrendered; Hickox wrote home that day. "This morning Col. Viel called . . . to announce the startling news . . . There have been meetings, etc., as to what everyone does. . . . We will continue as usual. Many rest camps will be set up, etc. The news didn't strike most of us much as there is still small scale fighting and conditions are about the same as they have been since the Rhine crossing."[25]

After the war, Hickox got some time off and traveled. She went to Scotland, Rome, and saw a Paris fashion show. But the war's effects were glaringly evident.[26]

"Munich is a shambles," she wrote on July 13, 1945. "It looks like droves of bombers just flew over and dumped their load. There isn't even a house or hotel intact." She also told about the father-in-law of her French friend, Pierre, who "aided some American aviators to escape in February 1944 and was arrested in August 1944 and taken to Buckenwald [sic] where he died just before the Americans arrived."[27]

Near the end of 1945 Hickox was promoted and started setting up American Red Cross clubs in Europe.[28]

"The American Red Cross is trying to close out here," she wrote on February 3, 1946. "The troops, too, are leaving." Her work there was winding down, too.[29]

The last item among Hickox's letters is a telegram dated April 24, 1946, from New York to her parents. It says, "Arrived safely . . . see you soon."[30]

REFERENCES

1. *Clarice Hickox, letter to parents, December 29, 1944.*
2. *Monica Mazzaro, interview with author, September 30, 2004.*
3. *Clarice Hickox, letter to parents, July 2, 1943.*
4. *Ibid.*
5. *Ibid.*
6. *Ibid.*
7. *Clarice Hickox, letter to parents, July 11, 1943.*
8. *Ibid.*
9. *Ibid.*
10. *Clarice Hickox, letter to parents, September 18, 1943.*
11. *Clarice Hickox, illustrated map.*
12. *Clarice Hickox, letter to parents, October 29, 1945.*

13. *Clarice Hickox, letter to parents, January 3, 1944.*
14. *Ibid.*
15. *Clarice Hickox, letter to parents, January 20, 1944.*
16. *Clarice Hickox, letter to father, January 13, 1945.*
17. *Ibid.*
18. *Ibid.*
19. *Ibid.*
20. *Clarice Hickox, self-written article included in letter to parents, April 28, 1945.*
21. *Ibid.*
22. *Clarice Hickox, letter to parents, March 5, 1945.*
23. *Ibid.*
24. *Clarice Hickox, letter to parents, April 28, 1945.*
25. *Clarice Hickox, letter to parents, May 7, 1945.*
26. *Clarice Hickox, letters to parents, May 10-July 2, 1945.*
27. *Clarice Hickox, letter to parents, July 13, 1945.*
28. *Clarice Hickox, letter to parents, December 2, 1945.*
29. *Clarice Hickox, letter to parents, February 3, 1946.*
30. *Clarice Hickox, telegram to parents, April 24, 1946.*

MY JOURNEY TO FREEDOM

by Jack Vogelsang
Oceanside, California
2004

I t was about sixty years ago in the former Dutch East Indies, now called Indonesia, that, in March 1947, almost two years after the end of the Japanese occupation during World War II, I regained my freedom after two years of imprisonment.

I was a fourteen-year-old boy when I was imprisoned, a third-generation Dutch citizen born in Batavia, now called Jakarta, Indonesia, where my family belonged to the middle class.

It was the Dutch nationality that placed me, my family, and many other people of Dutch nationality, in the predicament of persecution. From the onset of the Japanese occupation in 1942, thousands of Dutch citizens—men, women, and children—were declared *"musuh"* (enemy) by the Japanese and placed in concentration camps, where many died of starvation, disease, and execution.

I inherited my Dutch nationality from my father, and he, in turn, from his father and grandfather. According to Dutch law, the Dutch citizenship can only be attained through inheritance from the father's side or by dispensation.

According to my family's genealogical records[1], my great-grandfather, who was born in The Hague, Holland, in 1833, and who was a police provost by profession, had been assigned the post of provost in Batavia by the Dutch government. There, he married my great-grandmother, who was an Indonesian. He thus founded the Dutch-Indonesian branch and dual ethnicity of the family.

Our Dutch heritage included the Dutch nationality, the Reformed branch of the Christian religion, and the Dutch language, culture, and education, both in Indonesia and Europe. Indonesia is my land of origin, or Motherland, and Holland or The Netherlands, my Fatherland.

Until this day, even though I am an American citizen, and have lived in the U.S. for forty-six years and my children and grandchildren are U.S.-born citizens, I am still in many respects attached to Holland and Indonesia by culture, language, and family history.

THE REVOLUTION

When Japan capitulated in 1945, the Dutch East Indies was not liberated by any of the Allied armies from America, England, or Australia. Instead, the Japanese occupying armies just laid down their weapons at the command of their leaders, which created a power vacuum. The Allied High Command under General Douglas MacArthur ruled that England would take command of all of Southeast Asia, including the Dutch East Indies. Holland had just been liberated from German occupation and was not able to take control of their colony, the Dutch East Indies.

To maintain law and order, until such time that control of the country could be handed over to the postwar Dutch Government, England dispatched British Indian Army units, including the famous *Gurkhas*, to Java. These troops were stationed in three provincial capitals, Batavia, Semarang, and Soerabaya, located along the north coast of Java and around the interconnecting highways. A temporary government called NICA (Netherlands Indies Civil

Administration) was created and a demarcation line or border was drawn, creating a British-controlled enclave.

Soekarno, who had collaborated[2] with the Japanese during the occupation, called on the Indonesian people for the *Bersiap* (Call for Action) and the Indonesian people started a revolution for independence from the Dutch. This revolution lasted four years until 1949, when The Netherlands, under pressure from the U.S.A., granted Indonesia her independence.

Many Indonesians had been trained by the Japanese military to fight the Allies in case there was an invasion, and they had taken over the weapons and equipment from the Japanese. Peasants armed with machetes and bamboo spears went amok against the *Orang Blanda*, the Dutch, including the local-born people of Dutch descent. Many men, women, and children were butchered. There was anarchy and these Dutch civilians could not defend themselves. They had no weapons, nor the strength to fight. Many had survived the Japanese concentration camps. They were emaciated and were walking skeletons.

Soon, the Indonesian masses and "people's army," however ragged, took control of the rest of Java, which went with much terror, and butchery. All Dutch nationals, including the local-born, like myself, living in the regions controlled by the Indonesians, were rounded up and put in concentration camps. During the two years that we spent in these camps, we were moved at gunpoint by train, truck, or on foot, from one camp to another, where we existed in starvation, sickness, and misery.

As the revolution raged on, many of the Indonesian insurgents were captured by the Dutch military. Toward the end of 1946, a cease fire was called and the leaders of the warring parties agreed to exchange Indonesian prisoners against Dutch internees.

MY JOURNEY TO FREEDOM

The Indonesian military commander of our camp—which was called Klampok Banyuma and located deep in central Java—

informed us that we would be released and that a train would transport us to Batavia, the capital city. However, the move would be done in two phases, women and children first and men in alphabetical order. I fell in the second group of males because my last name started with a letter V, which meant that I would be released three or four months later.

Finally, in March 1947, the big day to freedom arrived. I was sixteen years old at that time. It was six years since the start of World War II, and almost two years since it ended. I had been separated from my family for two years and I did not know what had become of them, or whether they were dead or alive.

Little preparations for the move were necessary. We men and boys were naked except for a loincloth. That was all that was left of our worldly possessions.

It was about five o'clock in the afternoon and it was getting dark when we were ordered to board the train. The duration of the journey to Batavia was expected to be about twelve hours, barring unforeseen circumstances. The journey would lead us through mountainous and forested regions in politically and militarily contested territories. Communications between controlling revolutionaries was poor and primitive. The train could be highjacked, ambushed, or blown up by insurgents not informed of the agreed exchange and transportation of the ex-prisoners through their territory. There were no provisions for food or drinking water on the train.

It was raining hard when we stood in a single line to enter the decrepit and dilapidated old wooden train. Despite the rain and cold we were in a jubilant mood. There were about one hundred twenty of us in this last group of internees. We were divided in groups of twenty, and each group was directed to an assigned car. An armed Indonesian soldier, dressed in ragged clothing, stood guard at each end of the cars.

The train finally was set in motion toward freedom. We sat on long wooden benches along the windows. The rain poured into the cars through the open windows and through long holes in the roofs where the wooden planks had peeled off. We were wet and cold to the bones. Gradually, the joy, singing, and laughter ended. After hours of traveling, it stopped raining and the moon appeared through the clouds. It was quiet now, except for the monotonous rhythm of iron wheels rolling over the rails and the occasional wail of the locomotive's whistle.

I got up to stretch my back and limbs. Most of the people in the car were asleep. I walked toward the door and stepped on the platform. The armed guard leaned against the cast-iron railing, next to the hand wheel, which operated the brakes. He was smoking a cigarette. Each time he sucked a lungful of smoke, it caused the cigarette tip to light up brightly, which illuminated his face. As he exhaled, I smelled the pungent scent of clove in the smoke of typical Indonesian cigarettes. He was just a peasant, but nonetheless, inspired by his quest for independence. His young face fierce and determined. His long hair was blowing in the wind. The revolutionaries had vowed not to cut their hair until independence had been attained.

He looked at me and nodded with a faint smile.

I folded my arms across my naked chest and rubbed my upper arms. Then I rubbed my bare thighs and legs. The rushing air was cool but pleasant.

"May I sit on the steps?" I asked him in his native Malay language, and pointing to the steps of the old-fashioned car.

"Okay, but be careful," he answered.

I sat down on the car steps, stuck my left arm through the cast-iron railing, locking a bar in my arm. I held my wrist with my right hand.

The air was cool after the monsoon rain had stopped. As I sat on the car steps of the moving train, I took a deep breath, letting the wind blow in my face, and thought: "Finally, we are being freed," but actually not fully comprehending what it was going to be like or what the future would bring. After years of occupation, imprisonment, hunger, malnutrition, chronic malaria, and six years of no schooling, the future was dark. But the joy and promises of the moment overshadowed all worries.

As the train proceeded, I looked at the bright moon and stars appearing from behind the dark clouds and disappearing again, creating silver linings around massive cumulus clouds. The dark shadows and silhouettes of the trees along the tracks rushed by. The rhythmic motions of the car and the hypnotic sounds of the wheels on the rails rocked me to sleep . . . I dreamed of peace and freedom; that I was flying free with the wind rushing in my face and through my hair . . . I felt that I was falling . . .

A sudden jolt at my left arm and shoulder woke me up. My arm strapped around the railing bar had avoided my sleeping body from falling off the car steps into the abyss . . .

With my heart racing, but thankful that I had not fallen, I got up and went inside the car to continue my journey to freedom.

At about noon time the next day, we safely arrived in Batavia, where, after six long years, we saw the Dutch flag flying high.

Finally, freedom had become reality.

REFERENCES

1. Leeuwen, A.M.W. van, _Genealogy of the Vogelsang family in The Dutch East Indies_, Vlaardingen, The Netherlands, 2002.

2. Hering, Bob, _Soekarno, founding father of Indonesia, Royal Institute of Linguistics and Anthropology_, 2300 RA Leiden, The Netherlands, 2002.

Coda

The world is round
and the place which may seem like the end
may also be the beginning.
— Ivy Baker Priest

A Whole World of Choices

by Dorsetta Hale
Pacifica, California
2004

The white dress and shoes had been bought and the announcements sent. The final step was that walk down the aisle. And so it was, by the powers vested in the school system, our daughter is ready to graduate and go out into the world. I know that she is, but I still wonder.

As I stand in her room, careful not to crush the piles of CDs on the floor, my eyes search the walls for any sign of us. The posters of Bill Cosby reading to a group of children at the library and Martin Luther King, Jr. in profile were replaced long ago. One wall is dedicated to a singing group of five airbrushed and makeup-faced young white men wearing more earrings than I own. The other walls are covered with pictures of movie stars and scenes of Italy and Ireland.

Her black Barbies, Cabbage Patch, and Keisha dolls have been passed onto siblings. I still treasure my first black doll, because, when I was a child, my parents had two choices: blonde or brunette.

When I look at my daughter, I can't help but think of choices, the choices I made and those of my parents and of my parents' parents. My mother and father came from the South and lived in an all-black community. They fell in love young, got married, and moved almost 3,000 miles away so that I would have choices and better opportunities when I grew up.

It wasn't easy for them. The Bay Area was not the color-blind, rainbow paradise they expected. Since daddy "didn't sound black on the phone," each house he went to look at suddenly became unavailable. After weeks of frustration, he answered one ad and told the man straight up: "Look, I'm eighteen years old, I have a wife, and a newborn daughter. I have a job, I can afford the rent and I'm black. I don't want to waste your time or mine, can I see the house?" The voice on the other end of the phone line told him to come right over. That landlord and my father became lifelong friends.

If my daughter has been reluctant to learn the gory details of her ancestry, I can understand why, because I've been there. For a long time, I didn't want to know any more about how much my people suffered. A child can only take so many images of men hanging from trees and people being attacked by police dogs and hosed down with water by firemen. You want to learn something good, because the bad is never all there is.

In the seventh grade, after growing up in an all-white town, only seeing black people on the news and at church in Marin City on the weekends, I decided to take a new black-history class being offered at my school in San Anselmo. Mr. Cooper, whom I admired for his youth, long hair, corduroy pants, and general hipness, taught it. One day during class, he suggested that I most likely had Caucasian blood in me because "your hair is long, your skin is not dark, and it is a fact that female slaves were routinely raped by their masters and bred to produce more slaves." Although he was right, I remember shaking with rage. It was all I could do to keep from crying as my classmates turned to stare at me.

That night at home I asked my father, who had just earned his barber's license, to cut my hair into an Afro. My poor mother had to leave the room when she saw the hair she'd spent hundreds of hours pressing to make straight piled on the floor.

To paraphrase James Brown and Sly Stone, I was "black and proud and thank you for lettin' me be myself."

I guess I have my dad to thank for that. He was the proudest man I've ever known. Being black seemed to make him stronger. The way he spoke of the slaves who struggled to keep their dignity, whose children went on to raise families, become soldiers, teachers, doctors, inventors; it was as though we were related. It made me feel secure because I was connected. I began to understand why people referred to each other as brother or sister.

Whenever a Sidney Poitier movie, civil rights program, or Mohammed Ali boxing match would come on television, he made sure I watched it. He made sure I knew the history of rock 'n' roll and that Elvis and Pat Boone and others weren't doing anything Fats Domino, Little Richard, and others hadn't done before. He excused the Rolling Stones because they were cool and gave credit where credit was due. I could identify, because it was common knowledge that the Osmonds had no act without the Jackson Five.

Dad told me about race movies—movies written, acted, direct-ed, and produced by blacks. They played in theaters owned by black people. It was the same with schools, hospitals, and entire commu-nities. It was the life he lived in the segregated South.

To put it into perspective for me, he'd take us back to Alabama every summer. The experience always made me glad to get back to the Bay Area. In California, Daddy didn't need to carry a gun in the glove compartment of the car, and we didn't have to keep still and look straight ahead as we had to do when we drove through Mississippi.

In the South, there were signs everywhere that read, "Colored Only" this, "Whites Only" that. It was another world to me. Two other worlds. For me, coming from my neighborhood, the black world of Walco and Good Water was like coming home. The peo-ple knew my parents and respected me for being my father's daugh-ter. It filled me with pride that was about more than being black. Although he was the center of the universe that was my family, it amazed me that anyone else would think of him as special. But he was.

He wore *dashiki* shirts handmade by my mother long after they went out of style. After work, he was home for dinner at six o'clock on the dot. He didn't smoke, drink, or swear, and didn't allow anyone else to do so in front of us. He thought Mama was the greatest. Even Sophia Loren, whom daddy considered the second most beautiful woman on Earth, couldn't compare to her.

I remember him touching Mom all the time, holding hands in public and calling her Gerty Baby, which was nowhere near her real name. I never saw him drive without one arm wrapped around her shoulder on the bench seat of our Buick. For his love, I would have been proud, no matter what color he was.

On my daughter's desk is a copy of an essay she's written for a college entrance application. It's all about the man she called Granddaddy. It's an eloquent piece filled with love and pride for the man she spent every weekend and summer with, who told her the same stories he'd told me and even went so far as to take her back home to a changing South.

As I pick up her CDs and place them on her desk, I notice a pile of magazine photos of Samuel L. Jackson, Queen Latifah, Lauren Hill, Dorothy Dandridge, and others. There is also a cutout of a comic strip called "The Boondocks," about an overzealous, proud, young black boy who is trying to teach everyone—whether they want to or not—to learn from history. And I notice a sparse corner on the wall by her bed where these items will just fit. I realize that she's still growing, still learning, and I hope that when she looks at her father and me, she sees herself, the past and the future, and finds strength in the memory of those who made her choices possible.

She's been accepted to a university of her choice and will go there with the help of a scholarship created by a white man who was inspired by a black teacher. She plans to study film production. We look forward to seeing in theaters everywhere a film by my daughter, written, directed, and produced by a most colorful cast of human beings.

MY MOTHER IS A COPPER POT

by Phyllis I.T. Harris
Ames, Iowa

My mother is a copper pot of orange and pink and purple zinnias.
She is a 1913 passport upon which is penned
by someone in authority after "lips": medium.
She's a Swedish tea ring,
prime rib with garlic,
jeweled pomegranate seeds sprinkled on grapefruit.
She is all the letters she wrote placed end to end,
reaching round the earth.

My father is a stack of journals, squeezing out the umbrellas
in their very own hall closet. He is starched collars,
Panamas and straw hats. He's a quart jar of peaches
lifted from his mother's kitchen,
devoured behind his father's barn.
He is *101 Best Poems*.
He's the United Nations flags presented to the church
and to the library. He's Dag Hammarskjöld's *Markings*

presented to high school seniors.

My sister is a borrowed bird's nest,
a lover of animals, swimming,
with a mental disease that will kill her.
My sister is her sons, genetically afflicted,
gone.

My maternal grandmother is a handmade rag doll
with exquisite, embroidered features.
She's jet beads, a seal cape
and a crude hearing device that insults the fragile chest
it rests against under her thin blouse.

My maternal grandfather is a black lacquered tin box
trimmed in gold for receipts and his endless ciphers
during the Depression.
He's white bread and butter with sugar on it for fussy
grandchildren.
He's doubled vision driving us home in the dust
on gravel roads from the farm.

My paternal grandmother is a photograph in grays
in a gold frame on my father's bureau.
She's lumpy oatmeal my mother disdained for her infants.
She's a $400 bond willed to my sister before I was born
that she discovered, exchanged for a fur coat
without our father's knowledge.

My paternal grandfather is his paper of naturalization
from Northern Ireland.
He's the custard pie left him by his family
escaping a raid by the Sioux
before he joins his regiment in the Union Army.
He's the pitchfork, readied for protection

during the night alone in the barn.
He's brass surveying instruments.
He's pen and ink as county clerk and free railroad passes
as state legislator.

My great maternal grandmother is twelve inches of diaries
on the shelf, 1860-1906, widowed by a sawmill accident
in upstate New York, married in Illinois to
Patrick Henry Burchard, a sterling serving knife,
awarded for excellence in butter
at the Philadelphia Exposition of 1876.

My great, great maternal grandmother is a slender leather volume
of genealogy; poetry: "Beautiful Things," "The Heart's Index,"
"The Philosopher's Stone," "Saws for the Millions";
recipes for "cholera prevention," "constipation"
and "cheap but excellent ink."

My great, great maternal grandfather is a Samuel Terry
wooden works clock from the War of 1812
for which he traded a sheep
when steel belonged to the enemy.

I am the sum of these things and newspaper clippings, letters,
marks on the backs of receipts, road maps, photographs,
No. 2 pencils, scissors, stoked by heat from the past,
preserved with words.

MY MOTHER, THE STORYTELLER

by Maria B. Murad
Apple Valley, Minnesota
2004

I have a picture of my mother, which was taken around 1912. I guess she's about fifteen in it, but it's hard to pin down her age—she tended to put her own spin on most facts, her birth date included. She's holding an open parasol, and her cousin, May Arnett, holds an umbrella. She told me they decided as a lark to have the photo taken. They look so solemn, but I suspect they giggled when it was over. The parasol was an artsy prop the photographer had in his shop, although young ladies of this period often used them on sunny days to protect themselves from sunburn.

My mother, Ethel Ann, was the daughter of John Agnew Lowe and Maria Murphy Lowe (that's pronounced the Irish way: Mari'ah, with a long "i"). Johnny Lowe was a towering Scots from Glasgow, who worked on the railroad as an inspector. He loved to drink with his friends, and he was free with the dollar. He didn't leave much to his widow when he died of kidney failure. And there were lots of mouths to feed: He and Maria (tiny, barely five-foot tall, gentle

Maria) had: Mamie, Bud, Agnes, Charlotte, Alice, Harry, Frank, Grover, and Ethel.

Ethel was the youngest girl, the prettiest, the most petted by her father. He doted on her and called her "Pocahontas," because of her long, straight, blue-black hair. Her eyes were a dark hazel and in her early years, before she gained weight and suffered much illness and disillusionment, she was an absolutely classical beauty. Perfect nose, high cheekbones, gorgeous pale skin. She sat for an artist once, for a magazine cover. ("It went out of business after the first month," she used to say wryly.) My eldest daughter has that portrait hanging in her home now. The Irish was dominant in her. She was witty and bright and a wonderful storyteller, and when her father died when she was fifteen, she simply dropped the Scots part of her heritage, piqued, I think, because he dared to desert the family so abruptly.

Her mother came to the United States by way of Ireland (Armagh County, where St. Patrick established himself) and Nova Scotia. The Murphy family settled in La Crosse, Wisconsin, and were evidently well-to-do until the father died, leaving a naive widow who was easily bilked out of her property. Or so the story went from my mother. I am hazy about any relatives still in Wisconsin. I know the Arnett family was one, and Maria did have a brother and a sister-in-law in Minneapolis. There was a time when the family lived in St. Paul, and then, following John Lowe's railroad job, they moved up north, to a town above Duluth called Knife River. They later moved back to Duluth.

When my children were small, they used to ask me what I did when there was no television or videos. They used to stare at me in awe when I told them, well, I read, or I played with my dolls, or I listened to the radio: *Superman* and *Captain Midnight* after school, *Let's Pretend* on Saturday mornings. But what I forgot to tell them was that my brother and I used to listen for hours to my mother tell stories about "the olden days." It's a cliche to say she was Irish and had the gift of blarney, but she was Irish and she did have the gift of blarney.

She was a wonderful storyteller, possessing a talent for richness of detail and images, able to tell the most prosaic tales with dramatic pauses and a great sense of timing. She used to embellish a lot, but she never forgot the plot line or failed to end with a good, punchy finish. From her rich repertoire, my brother and I could select any kind of story we wanted—sentimental, funny, spooky, or sad. I always liked the sad ones best (being always a trifle morbid) but my brother liked the more outrageous ones that left him literally rolling on the floor with laughter. Being the elder, he usually got to pick first, but when my mother and I were alone and she was in a nostalgic mood, I got the kind I felt were more satisfying.

"Tell me about Bud," I'd say, and she'd be off, describing her oldest brother who died tragically after a skating mishap. Or she'd tell me about her friend, Hannah, who died of pneumonia when they were both children in Knife River, Minnesota. She'd tell me about her mother, Maria Murphy, my namesake, a tiny woman who had nine children with her big, gruff Scots husband who had emigrated from Glasgow. Always kind, religious, patient, Maria would chide her loud, overly generous husband with gentle admonitions: "Oh, Johnny . . ." was all she'd say.

When my grandmother died, my mother told me, a great crowd came to her funeral, including tradespeople and workmen who said she was the "salt of the earth."

Without too much urging, my mother used to talk a lot about her brother Grover, with whom she had shared an almost mystical association, so close were they. She attributed it to the fact that while they were eleven months apart in age, they had been born in the same year: she in January, he the following December. My mother always insisted that she had "The Second Sight," or "The Gift," as the Irish say. When Grover was taken ill on the streets of Minneapolis, she told me she just knew long before the police called her that something was wrong with him. It was a feeling so strong she couldn't shake it. He'd been stricken with heat exhaustion after a day of working in the yard, and he died within hours of his collapse.

I call it ESP, but whatever the name, it was a peculiarly Celtic attribute. A premonition of a death, a tragedy about to unfold, something unhappy in the atmosphere that announced itself to her silently but knowingly. I never doubted her because I, too, have this gift, as do some of my daughters. It manifests itself in different ways to different people, but it never seems scary or over the top to me. It just is.

So we listened, my brother and I, to old stories of people long dead and relatives who had bequeathed a rich heritage to us. I can see this cast of characters still in my mind. With her stories, she left us a great legacy of imagination. One of my daughters believes still in fairies and the little people, and unicorns who race across misty meadows. Even my most practical child has odd dreams that portend events, which come unbidden in her sleep. The Irish are the keepers of dreams and legends and I'm grateful for the gifts my mother bequeathed me. I, too, am a storyteller, though written skills, not oral, are my medium.

STORIES MY MOTHER
NEVER TOLD ME

by Victoria Law
New York, New York
2004

I n the preliterate past, history was committed to memory and passed down through stories and song. But what happens when the young cease to listen, when their minds wander as they fidget during grandmother's visit or auntie's recollection? What happens to history then?

My own mother was not a listener. If the story did not concern her, she let her mind drift. To whom, then, did her mother pass on the family stories and secrets? Or was my grandmother also not a listener? Did she squirm and fidget when her own mother tried to pass on the family heritage?

I piece together small pieces that my mother has let slip.

Her father was a manufacturer of coarse cloth bags used for shipping. He and his wife were Hakka, originally from a village called Meixian, and before that from places unknown. The tradition for women was to have unbound feet at a time when the crippled, curled lotus was still fetishized, and to wear broad-brimmed black fringe hats as they labored outside. I don't know if my mother's mother ever wore such a hat, and the pictures, if any even existed, have been buried away in a forgotten box.

I know that when the Japanese invaded China, her mother took her children and fled from village to village. One son was born in Guilin. But Guilin, with its pointed peaks and winding Lijiang River, also proved unsafe and so the family moved again and my mother was born in crowded Canton.

When the Communists came to power, the family fled to Hong Kong, leaving behind the three eldest daughters. Two eventually joined them. The third, who had been given away, my mother does not remember. The two youngest were born on Queen Victoria's barren rock. My grandfather did not prosper with the island; my mother's strongest memory is of eating peanuts with chopsticks, one at a time and slowly to make them last longer.

The two eldest daughters came and left. The eldest married a merchant from Indonesia, worked alongside him, and raised their seven children in Jakarta.

The next sister married a Chinese from South Africa who had come to Hong Kong simply to seek a wife. My mother remembers him as a strong, tall man who would let her and her brother dangle from his outstretched arms. Once he brought them an identical pair of chicks. They fought over one, claiming it looked more lively than the other. My aunt returned with him to South Africa where she learned enough English first to visit the ships docking in Durban to take the sailors' orders for supplies, then later to become the family raconteur. Over coffee or dinner or wine, she would tell us stories about her children or narrate the story of her sister who was given to another family in China. Her chattiness is a stark contrast to the silence of my mother's house. My aunt's words slowly fill the gaps and scrub the edges of the family question marks.

She and her husband lived with his parents, his brothers and their wives, and his sister, the first Chinese ever admitted to a South

African medical school.

My aunt raised two children in this house. Her son read and studied beneath the hallway of the dim light. Once, for Christmas, she and her husband bought him a horsehair brush. More than thirty years later, he still talks excitedly about the gift. Her daughter married a man from Taiwan, gave up her medical practice, and, with the help of the African maid who had left her own daughter to work for her, raised their two daughters.

The next sister, seeing the harshness of her sisters' lives, vowed not to marry a man without a college education. She knew one boy, the son of a Chinese man and his French wife. The boy moved to Canada and wrote her a letter. She never responded. And she never married. She lived with her parents and her youngest brother, watching first her father, then her mother die. Then she followed, having kept silent for too long about the lump growing in her breast.

My mother said that this sister had always kept quiet about her troubles. When she was a child, she would refuse to eat when angry. At a table full of hungry children and not enough food, no one noticed that her plate remained untouched. She always prepared the chicken, slicing its head off, then instructing my mother to hold the body above a bowl to catch the blood dripping from the severed neck. One day my mother realized that the corpse was still twitching and, although she had performed the task many times before, dropped the chicken. Blood and feathers splattered the floor. "Useless!" my aunt had screamed and never trusted her sister with the job again.

My mother says little about her own mother, a woman separated from me by a continent, an ocean, a language, and later, by death. As a child, my mother paid no attention to her words and stories and so can only pass on the bits and pieces that pertain to her. She was her father's favorite, and so it is he that she remembers. My mother can tell me virtually nothing about her own mother. Who was her mother's favorite? What was their relationship like? This story has long been buried with her mother.

I never questioned or even thought about my mother's silence until I left her house. Only then did I realize that I was missing the sense of identity that comes from family and personal history. Whenever someone begins a tale or shares a memory my ears prickle, my fingers itch for pen and paper, and my mind scrambles to commit it all before the words evaporate.

My mother did not leave me a legacy of words. So I stitch one together, weaving in not only those of my family but also of my community, to hand down to my own daughter and others, who, like me, grew up in silence.

THE FAMILY BUSINESS

by Laurie Levinger
Norwich, Vermont
2004

M y mother's people were in business. Her father, Schlomo (later he would change it to Sam), was a poor Jewish boy who grew up on the Lower East Side. He didn't have money, but what he did have was plenty of *chutzpah*. He married young, borrowed $500 from the neighborhood green grocer, which felt like a fortune to him, and started a paint business. Borrowing to finance a dream, it was a common enough story for those times. What was uncommon was what came next.

The company he started prospered so he and his new wife, Crystal (she started life as Goldie), emerged from the Depression having made, not lost, a small fortune.

They left their class behind without looking back once. They had achieved their fantasy, the American dream. *Nouveau riche*— even the term jingled like money—Grandpa Sam cast his eye about for a new challenge and found it in politics. He ran for office and eventually was elected mayor of their small town, near enough to

New York City to have a noticeable Jewish minority, but provincial enough to still be solidly anti-Semitic.

As mayor, Sam had the status he craved. He escorted his stylish wife and five small children to synagogue on the High Holidays, more to show off their holiday finery and to *kibbitz* with his political cronies than out of any religious conviction. He'd won as a Democrat, but party affiliation wasn't what was important. Learning the ropes, exercising influence, that was what demanded Sam's attention. But he was new to power; who knows what he did to cause relations with the local police union to sour? Maybe nothing, maybe he was just a Jew.

Early one sunny Monday morning after his five children had left for school, a disgruntled policeman shot Sam in front of his own house. Witnesses heard the officer screaming, "Jew-bastard!" and came running. They saw White—that was the enraged cop's name—kicking my grandfather long after the gun hung empty in his hand. Standing around what was now a corpse, they watched helpless, as Grandpa Sam's blood seeped into the pavement.

Sam died young, leaving behind an even younger wife and the children he had never taken the time to know, too busy making money, exercising power.

After two previous attempts (failures) to produce a son, my mother, Gloria, came along, having committed the original sin of not being a boy, and her father, Sam, had never let her forget it. She was fifteen when her father died on the sidewalk of the street that would bear his name as a permanent memorial.

Sam had earned a reputation as a bit of a conniver who hoarded his money, hoping to avoid taxes or provide for his family, it wasn't clear which. Anyway, he'd had the foresight to consult lawyers to plan for the future he'd never see, placing the business in trust for us, the as-yet-unborn grandchildren. That's what we heard when we were growing up: "The business belongs to the grandchildren." We didn't know what it meant exactly, but it sounded tantalizing. Someday we'd be business owners, too.

My father's people were intellectuals and writers; teaching and writing was their family business. Grandfather Solomon was a minor author, whose money-making job was working for the Jewish Welfare Board. Grandmother Esther wrote prolifically. Both were "Jewish writers," focusing on Jewish history, philosophy, and biographies of famous Jews.

Like Grandpa Sam, my Grandfather Solomon grew up poor. He didn't dream of money, he devoted his energies to getting an education, earning a full scholarship and a PhD in philosophy, unusual for anyone, but especially a poor Jew in the early 1900s. Craving the title "professor," he longed to teach, but since there weren't any university jobs, he'd had to settle for becoming a rabbi. When the reality that he couldn't find work dawned, he volunteered for the Army, serving in France during the First World War, a chaplain to boys in the trenches. He wrote a book about his war experiences, never mentioning that while he was ministering to injured or dying Jewish boys, his wife was home, grieving the death of one of their infant twins, the baby Moses, during the flu epidemic of 1918. My grandmother survived, but she was never right afterwards.

The living twin, Judith, was bereft her entire life.

Grandmother Esther's books were not esoteric, containing little philosophy or theory. Instead, she aimed at making Jewish education entertaining and engaging, a novel approach in those days. She didn't "have a job"—she stayed at home with her children, of course—but found time to write more than twenty biographies, plays, and children's books. We had two entire shelves of books by Levingers in the bookcases that lined our family room.

My mother tolerated Grandfather Solomon, and, though she didn't much like him, she forced herself to take good care of him during his last years, when he came to live with us. But she hated my grandmother. I don't know how I knew this exactly. She certainly never said so directly. But I inhaled the hate when I breathed; it was in the air.

In part, she blamed Esther for what she felt was wrong with my father—that he wasn't very communicative or warm. Later on, after all us kids had left home and she was alone with my father, she got fed up with his silences. She would command, "Speak to me, oh sage," equal parts admiration and goading. He'd look stumped, and then come up with some comment or other, hoping it would satisfy. She described all the Levingers—my father, his sister, and their parents—as "too goddamn intellectual." Said they "cared about all the wrong things."

Many years later, she told me stories that helped fill in some of the blanks. All the episodes were really variations of the same basic tale. This particular one sums it up best: Grandmother Esther was visiting us at our house outside Jackson, Mississippi, where we moved when my father got his first university job.

My mother had her hands full. She was pregnant with me, constantly nauseous from the misnamed morning sickness. She spent most of her time trying not to throw up, struggling to keep up with my brother, Benny, her first-born, a wiry, energetic four-year-old.

Names had weight in our family. Benny was named for my father's brother, Benjamin, Grandmother Esther's oldest son. A mythological figure, he'd volunteered to fight with the Abraham Lincoln Brigade during the Spanish Civil War and was killed in Spain, just twenty years old. He'd been a writer, too, sending home stories and poems so vivid they made his comrades, the Spanish resistance, and even the countryside come alive. Benjamin was an unspoken presence, looming yet invisible—the family hero, what we should all aspire to—but my father never really told us much about him. Except that he ran away when he was fourteen, and when he was brought back home, he became the fastest long-distance runner his high school had ever seen. My father was fifteen when his brother died fighting the good fight.

That history hovered over little Benny's head. When my father arrived home from the train station with my grandmother, my mother woke Benny from his nap.

"They're here, it's time to say hello to your grandma."

Jerking awake, Benny ran, skipping, leaping, flying down the driveway to welcome her. Benny was a fast runner, too, and Brownie, the family dog, trotted along, trying to catch up, sharing the excitement. My mother trailed behind, watching proudly.

Grandmother Esther bent down, her arms stretched open, cooing, "Oh, oh, isn't he cute."

With that, she threw her arms around the little brown dog, greeting him with kisses.

My mother never got over it.

I started to write when I was seven, poetry mostly. But it was a secret compulsion, a private pleasure. I wrote bits and scribbles—often started, but left unfinished--on the backs of envelopes and in journal after spiral-bound journal, for the next thirty years. I didn't show my scribbling to anyone. Worry panted down my neck when I wrote: It wasn't clear what exactly could be said and what couldn't. Could I fictionalize enough to tell all the stories that were begging to be told?

What I did know with utmost clarity was that writing was a risky proposition, I might violate unwritten rules. I couldn't afford to take chances. I loved my mother desperately. How could I be a writer?

I can see now, looking back, that I studied psychology, became a psychotherapist, practiced "the talking cure," to try to help other people tell their stories. And I was pretty good at it. Hundreds of stories later, after uncounted hours of listening, unanticipated circumstances collided, forcing me into an early retirement.

Untethered from my career and my identity as a listener, I foundered, searching for work that would be engaging, challenging, right for me.

Maybe my appointment with Vincent, the psychic I'd consulted when I turned forty, maybe that consultation opened me, paving the way for Dorothy, the latest in a long string of therapists.

Dorothy talked about past lives and nodes conjuncting, she was "centered," and assured me that when I finished counseling with her I'd arrive at my own centering, having discovered what my new right work was. Silently, I scoffed, despairing. I couldn't imagine I'd ever find other work that I would care about as much. Or be as good at.

Dorothy required that all her clients write, as well as talk. Writing was not optional.

For two years I wrote every day, filling page after page, note-book after notebook. When I was done with therapy-writing, I couldn't stop. I started to write short stories—very short—and when I was finished with those, I discovered I wanted to write longer ones. I wasn't convinced I had anything much to say, so those longer stories were still brief, strangely truncated. But the actual fact of creating them was satisfying beyond my wildest imaginings.

Dorothy was on the money. By the time my work with her was done, I understood that my future was about going back to pick up dropped stitches. Right work or not, this had become a necessity, driven by an almost physical urgency. The threat: tsunami or vol-cano? Water or fire? Inside or outside? The risks, the consequences, of stepping over some invisible boundary and landing in one of the swamps I had spent my life tiptoeing around, that still loomed. But I really didn't have a choice anymore. I had to do it, it was in my blood. Because now, I could not not write.

WHAT IS THE POINT?

by Elizabeth George
San Francisco, California
2003

Genealogy. What is the point? A bunch of names and dates: born, died, children. Boring—yawn. Maybe good for a little coffee-break conversation.

"Oh, yes, I can trace my ancestors back to 1675"

"Wow, 1675? Is that right? Anybody famous?"

"Well . . . no . . ."

So much for that. Who wants to hear about a bunch of regular folks?

One morning, I got up early to visit the porcelain parlor and caught my reflection passing the medicine cabinet. My mother was standing where I should have been.

Scared the s*** out of me (pardon my French).

I avoided mirrors altogether for several days after that. When I finally got the nerve to look again, she was still there. On closer inspection, so was my dad, grandpa, and grandma. Freaky, they all fit in my own fairly normal-sized face.

I worried about this for weeks. I'm me, dammit! Totally unique and individual! (I have spent forty years proving it.) Eventually, I decided it didn't matter. So what if my face had turned out to be just an amalgam of genetic bits of others? My face might not be an original, but my personality is still all me. They can't be in there, too, can they? (Although that would explain . . . so many things.)

So, then it was me that wanted to hear about a bunch of regular folks. (After all, if we were all going to live in this body of mine, we might as well at least know each other's names.) I brought the old photo albums out of the cupboard, and the genealogy my great-aunt had given me back in the '80s. I gathered up every bit of family memorabilia I could find; and I went to the library with it.

I didn't go to the big, new, flashy library downtown. I didn't go to the one with the banks of computer screens and video terminals. I went to the little one by the edge of the city; the one I heard was a "genealogy library." The one with only ten parking spaces and five of them are empty. The library that has the old-fashioned bus lockers in the entryway, where you must leave all the modern conveniences of life locked up. The library that only allows you to enter with the clothes on your back and a pencil and notebook in your hand, stripped down to the basics of research—no coffee allowed, and the peanut-butter sandwich stays in the locker.

I lost myself in that library for days on end. I became "one of them" when I was there, although I was at least twenty years younger than most of the other patrons. We all walked slowly, breathed heavily, and choked back tears when familiar names appeared in ancient tomes. I relearned how to use microfilm, microfiche, and a card catalog on index cards. I touched, with my own hands, a book that was written before 1800, the librarian actually allowed me to turn the brittle and stained pages and read the hand-printed text of a book more than two hundred years old.

And they were there, my ancestors. I found them in the old records, and I found them in myself. I recognized in the characters of the past the characteristics of the present. The spunk, the contrariness, the bravery, the creativity, the pride, the self-sufficiency, they were repeated again and again. No, there were none famous, but heroics abounded. The adventures of birth, loves, and death were there. The adversities of every-day life and the transgressions and redemptions of "regular folks' " family life were there, as they are now.

Before I was old enough to understand or care, grandpa told me that one of the tragedies of modern society is the broken link from one generation to the next.

"Things were going on, people were living, dying, loving, even as much as 8,000 years ago, and our past goes through all those generations."

He said, "They are, altogether, you, what you are and what you think, it is in essence your ancestors."

It is true, what I am is inextricably tangled in the web of those I came from.

And that is the point.

About the Authors

MELODY AMSEL-ARIELI, MAALEH ADUMIN, ISRAEL

Raised in rural New Jersey, Ms. Amsel-Arieli teaches flute and writes in Jerusalem, Israel. Her essays appear frequently in publications across America. Her study of Slovakian Jews, <u>Between Galicia and Hungary: The Jews of Stropkov</u> (Avotaynu, 2002), is held by many institutions, including Columbia University, UCLA, Yale University, University of Chicago, Princeton University, University of Oxford (UK), and Yad VaShem, the Holocaust Martyrs' and Heroes' Remembrance Authority of the State of Israel.

FRANK F. V. ATKINSON, CANBERRA, AUSTRALIA

Frank Atkinson is a retired Australian biologist/toxicologist and is interested in bird photography and genealogy. Frank's family name runs back to 1650-1800 in Lympley Stoke, Wiltshire, England, where it was Atkins. When James Atkins married in 1830, it became Atkinson. His mother's Jewish line has been traced back to a 1799 marriage in the Great Synagogue in London, with Sephardic connections from Jamaica. Frank has a grandfather buried in Los Angeles, California, U.S.A.

LIBBY ATWATER, VENTURA, CALIFORNIA

Ms. Atwater is a journalist, teacher, and personal historian who has written extensively for non-profit organizations, educational institutions, magazines, community newspapers, and businesses. She began recording life stories in 1997, and then added teaching classes in life writing and ethical wills to her offerings. She has written and edited several personal and family-history books, has composed a corporate legacy statement for a family-owned business, and is a member of the Association of Personal

233

Historians (*www.personalhistorians.org*), and the *American Tribute Center* (*www.tributecenter.org*), and an affiliate of the *Soleil Lifestory Network* (*www.turningmemories.com*) and The *Legacy Center* (*www.thelegacycenter.net*). The article in this book, <u>A Worthwhile Search</u>, will eventually be part of a longer work, <u>My Three Mothers: The Holy Trinity</u>.

MARY JANE BATTAGLIA, PLACERVILLE, CALIFORNIA

"Genealogical curiosity nipped me at a very early age," Ms. Battaglia writes. "I used to crawl under my grand-mothers' quilting frames and hide there, listening to the grownups exchange family gossip while they stitched. Over time, I've been able to flesh out and document most of what I heard—plus more! It has been my pleasure, as an avid student of history, to be able to place my own ancestors in actual historical settings!"

RITA BERMAN, CHAPEL HILL, NORTH CAROLINA

Ms. Berman was born in London, and emigrated to the U.S., where she became a freelance writer and lecturer. During a thirty-year career, she has published almost five hundred travel and feature articles in diverse publications in England and the U.S. She writes: "Family history is of great interest to me. ... I began writing my memoirs when Tess Booker, my granddaughter, asked what was it like to be a little girl in England. The contest entry (<u>I Saw London Burning</u>) is part of a much larger work."

MARLENE BROOKS BRANNON, CARLSBAD, CALIFORNIA

"My interest in genealogy stems from work done by my late sister. Until her death, I had been content to let her to do research while I basked in the knowledge. My first love, though, is writing. I've had several pieces published, and two of my works will appear in <u>Tidepools</u>, pub-

*lished by Mira Costa College, where I've received an
award for excellence in the category of literature. I also
write a regular newspaper column, Senior Update, for
San Diego North County Times."*

ANDREA BUTLER-RAMSEY, BRONX, NEW YORK

*Ms. Butler-Ramsey has pursued her passion for genealogy for
over twenty years. She is a member of the Afro-American
Historical & Genealogical Society (AAHGS) and the Jean
Sampson Scott Greater New York (JSSNY) local chapter, and
has contributed articles to the newsletters of both. Her involve-
ment in the JSSNY-AAHGS has included serving as chairper-
son of the Caribbean Committee, participating as an instructor
in the Girl Scout Heritage Seminars held at Barnard College in
New York, and as a member of the Writer's Group. Ms.
Butler-Ramsey has completed the National Genealogical Society
Genealogy Home Study Course, and contributed to the NGS
Quarterly. In addition to repositories in the U.S., her research
and efforts to find and spiritually connect to her ancestors have
taken her to the Caribbean countries of Antigua, Barbados, St.
Lucia, and the U.S. Virgin Islands, as well as the Public
Record Office in Kew, Richmond Surrey, England, and to sever-
al countries on the West Coast of Africa. She strongly believes
in passing on the information she has compiled, and to this end
has presented on various aspects of Caribbean research at the
AAHGS National Conferences, JSSNY-AAHGS local meetings and workshops, at the New York and Queens LDS Family
History Centers, and at the Smithsonian in Washington, D.C.
Ms. Butler-Ramsey has a master's degree in Art Therapy and
works full time as an art therapist in the Bronx. She is also a
mother and grandmother and enjoys painting and writing poetry.*

EMILY CARY, SCOTTSDALE, ARIZONA

*Ms. Cary inherited her love of genealogy from her mother, who
turned many family vacations into history quests and graveyard*

explorations. One journey to Pennsylvania traced ancestors who staked their claim by nicking trees with a tomahawk. This family's records and local folklore inspired one of Cary's mysteries, The Ghost of Whitaker Mountain (Thomas Bouregy, 1979; reprint, Ogden Press, 2002). She has also published The Pritchard Family History (Heritage Books, 2001), and articles in numerous magazines and newspapers, including The New York Times and The Philadelphia Inquirer.

ANNE CLARKE, CHRISTCHURCH, NEW ZEALAND

A fourth-generation New Zealander, Ms. Clarke grew up listening to stories about her family as told graphically by her father. It was not until she was in her mid-forties, when her father's memoirs were found and printed for her siblings, that her interest blossomed into family history studies. For more than twenty-five years, she has gathered information. She realized that her children and grandchildren may take a while to realize, as she did, that their heritage is not only important, but also extremely interesting. This has led her to write the stories, and produce books for the family, so that one day, they, too, can be amazed at the struggles, tragedies, delights, honours, and triumphs which the families lived through. She reports that she has no intention of slowing down her search for those elusive ancestors.

BONNIE COPELAND, COSTA MESA, CALIFORNIA

Ms. Copeland writes: "I thought all the stuff my parents and grandparents taught me was junk until I lived long enough to see its value." She has spent the twelve years since retirement sifting the wisdom and skills she learned from others through her own life experience and passing it on as a grandmother, volunteer business counselor with SCORE (Service Corps of Retired Executives), teacher of traditional women's crafts, and writer. Her two stories in this anthology are her first published works.

Margaret Cullison, Grants Pass, Oregon

Although she has lived in other states, Ms. Cullison claims Iowa as her birthright. A third generation Iowan, she grew up in the house where her father was born and lived out his life. Family stories fascinated her from an early age. The family home of over one hundred years holds a wealth of pictures, letters, diaries, and newspaper clippings from which she has gathered material for the essays she writes about her ancestors, her own childhood, and small-town life of earlier times. She now lives in Oregon and works as a freelance writer. Many of her essays are posted on Senior Women Web (http://www.seniorwomen.com/). An animal lover, she writes for trade magazines in the pet industry with her faithful Burmese cat, Kona, on her lap.

Gunter David, Fort Washington, Pennsylvania

Mr. David was a newspaperman on major U.S. city newspapers for twenty-five years, and was nominated for the Pulitzer Prize by the Philadelphia Evening Bulletin. With the demise of The Bulletin, he changed careers, and obtained a master's degree in family therapy and established a private practice. Now retired, he has published twenty short stories and memoirs in recent years, and lectures at Montgomery County Community College. He also contributes articles on mental and physical health to the Jewish Exponent, a Philadelphia weekly.

Michele Ivy Davis, Palm Harbor, Florida

Michele Ivy Davis was born in Washington, D.C., and went to nine different schools before she graduated from high school. As the child of a foreign service officer, she spent her junior high years in south India. Her writing has been published in Chicken Soup for the Sister's Soul, as well as numerous magazines and newspapers. Under the name Mickey Davis she writes articles for law-enforcement publications. Her novel Evangeline Brown and the Cadillac Motel was published in May 2004 by Dutton.

AARON L. DAY, LONG BEACH, CALIFORNIA

Mr. Day was born in Xenia, Ohio, and received a bachelor's degree in business administration; he has worked as an accountant most of his life. He has written columns for the Friends of the Long Beach Public Library, the NAACP Long Beach Branch, the California State Genealogical Alliance, and the Questing Heirs Genealogical Society. He has also published articles in Everton's Family History magazine and Heritage Quest, and appeared in several anthologies. He began family history research with his maternal side in the early 1980s, and began actively researching his father's side of the family in 1998. He has published two books: Locating Free African American Ancestors: A Beginner's Guide (2003) and History Lessons (2005).

AMY FALKENSTEIN, FAIRMONT, WEST VIRGINIA

Amy Williams Falkenstein writes that she is the mother of a little boy who will never know his great grandparents, his Great-Great-Aunt Ruth or Mrs. Wise from down the street, among many other pertinent yet deceased relatives/neighbors that Amy deems critical to her family's heritage. Her mission that they be real to her son, Nathan, began during her pregnancy, although she has been writing about her family, secretly, for years. She writes that she's "a sucker for love, good sentence structure, and tomato sandwiches."She teaches English part-time at Fairmont State University. Above all, she tells us, she "loves God."

HELEN KUEHN GAMELIN, PACIFIC PALISADES, CALIFORNIA

Ms. Gamelin grew up in San Carlos, California, and graduated from the University of California, Berkeley. When her four children went off to school, she enrolled in Santa Monica Community College, earned an RN degree, and worked for a period as a nurse. Her favorite activities are playing with her five grandchildren and gardening.

ELIZABETH GEORGE, SAN FRANCISCO, CALIFORNIA

Ms. George writes: "I began writing short stories when I was four years old and my mother presented me with art supplies in a vain attempt to gain a few minutes of peace from my constant chatter. To her dismay, I used the pencils and paper to draw complicated stories, which I then recited, out loud, of course. I am still a genealogy newbie, but I hope I never lose the excitement and anticipation that accompanies the slow and tedious unfolding of each ancestor's life story, and the honor and purpose I feel as I undertake to retell those stories."

DORSETTA HALE, PACIFICA, CALIFORNIA

Ms. Hale works full time as a 911 Public Safety Dispatcher. She lives in the Bay Area, and writes in between emergencies.

NORMA ANN HANSON, CLARKS GROVE, MINNESOTA

Ms. Hanson says that she became interested in family history as a teenager in the 1960s, asking her grandparents lots of questions, "which annoyed them no end—they thought I was quite a pest," she says. She put her interests in family history and writing aside for a number of years after she married and raised her children, but then began writing again about ten years ago. She says she has no plans to stop.

KENNETH F. HARRIS, TUSCON, ARIZONA

Mr. Harris writes: "Born in Southern California in 1933. A retired middle-school teacher with experience in California, Guam, and Spain. Also worked as a freelance writer, editor, and saloon singer. No longer writing for profit, just for fun, and for sharing with family. I believe you should write your own life story before you die and your rotten kids do it for you."

PHYLLIS I.T. HARRIS, AMES, IOWA

Phyllis Irene Thompson Harris has a BA from the University of Minnesota, an MEd from the University of Illinois, and an

MFA from Vermont College. She says she "likes to engage in time travel to the extent that I am able. . . . and [I] hope future generations in the family will be similarly enticed."

D. ELWERN JONES, DENBIGHSHIRE, NORTH WALES

Ms. Jones was born in St. Asaph, North Wales, and moved to Rhyl with her family when she was nine years of age. She followed a nursing career before marrying a Presbyterian minister in 1955. Her husband served as an Army chaplain for sixteen years, so they moved around a great deal, both in the U.K. and overseas. She writes: "Family history has been a hobby of mine since I was quite young—which has meant a great deal of researching both at home and abroad, and has been a means of making many very good friends over the years."

DIANE KOLB, MELROSE PARK, PENNSYLVANIA

Ms. Kolb is a Philadelphia native who began her writing career as a children's librarian and storyteller. She received her master's degree in Library and Information Science from Drexel University, and served as a children's librarian in both public and elementary school libraries. Her middle-grade novel, <u>My Father Is a Clown</u> (Publish America), was nominated for the 2003 Christopher Award. Her work has appeared twice on the children's pages of <u>Cat Fancy Magazine</u>, and has appeared as featured articles in other magazines. Her short stories have been included in <u>Haunted Experiences</u> (Atriad Press), and <u>Whose Panties Are These? More Misadventures From Funny Women on the Road</u> (Travelers' Tales, Inc., distributed by Publishers Group West). She has also co-authored <u>125 Bible Puzzles for Kids Ages 6-8</u> (Standard Publishing Co.). Her first illustrated picture-book story, "Fairy Boo-Boos," is featured in <u>Say Goodnight to Illiteracy 10th Anniversary Edition</u> (Halfprice books.com contest winner, 2004). Ms. Kolb is an active member of The Society of Children's Book Writers & Illustrators, and is a frequent speaker at schools and organizations.

JANICE LAPIDES, LA CAÑADA-FLINTRIDGE, CALIFORNIA
Ms. Lapides is the great-great-granddaughter of Robert Thornley, and the grand-niece of Wilson Robert Thornley. (See the biography of Wilson Thornley, the author of A Sketch of the Life of Robert Thornley.) She was raised on family stories and says she was thrilled when she found out that some had already been written down. Janis left her technical-writing profession to raise three children, and has since immersed herself in genealogy. She considers finding the stories behind the names of ancestors "the icing on the cake!"

VICTORIA LAW, NEW YORK, NEW YORK
Ms. Law comes from a family of non-talkers. Despite (or perhaps because of) this, she began writing. In 1998, she published Talk Story, a zine of family anecdotes based on a trip to Hong Kong in 1997. Since that time, she has also woven family history into her zines Dear Cookie: Postcards from Hong Kong and China and Dear Ms. Cookie: Postcards From an American-Born Chinese Visiting Her South African-Bred Cousins (or the Little Known Lore of the Chinese in South Africa). In addition to trying to record family history, she also writes about prison issues, particularly the concerns of women in prison, motherhood, and activism. She is also a documentary photographer, and is still trying to find a method of blending words and images to better tell (and retell) her stories.

GINA LEE, BURBANK, CALIFORNIA
Ms. Lee works at the Burbank Public Library and writes part-time. As a child, she says she loved listening to family stories, and was particularly fascinated by the grandmother who is the subject of her article in this anthology—"because we looked so much alike." She started building a family tree when she was about nine, and "just kept adding to it as she found out more information."

LAURIE LEVINGER, NORWICH, VERMONT

Laurie Levinger is a retired psychotherapist who lives and writes in Norwich, Vermont. The Family Business (page 223), is a chapter from her as-yet-unpublished memoir, Dropped Stitch. She writes that she is intrigued by the way family patterns are woven across generations, emerging in an individual life.

TARA MCCLELLAN MCANDREW, SPRINGFIELD, ILLINOIS

Ms. McAndrew is the local-history columnist for the Springfield, Illinois, daily newspaper, the State Journal-Register. She has been a freelance writer and broadcast journalist for nineteen years. Her articles have been published in more than thirty-five international, national, and local publications and her radio programs have been broadcast on Illinois Public Radio and National Public Radio. She has also written a few short plays about women from history, including one about the abolitionist Grimke sisters. One side of her family dates back four generations in central Illinois, which partly explains her passion for its fascinating history.

DENNIS MCCARGAR, TUJUNGA, CALIFORNIA

Mr. McCargar was born in Nebraska, and graduated from high school in Colorado. He was a music major in college, before enlisting in the Navy. He has earned two MA s, one in history and one in library science, and has taught (history, music, Spanish, genealogy, and economics), been an archivist, a miner, truck driver, Port of Entry officer, and driver instructor, among other occupations. He was employed by the California Department of Corrections for eleven years, and is now the reference librarian at the L.A. County Library in Baldwin Park. He says he has been interested in genealogy since he was nineteen.

MARIA B. MURAD, APPLE VALLEY, MINNESOTA

Ms. Murad has published a children's book, short stories, and essays, and is currently revising a novel. She is particularly interested in memoirs as a way to preserve the legacy of her family. She has written extensively about her Irish mother and her Italian father so that her children and grandchildren will have an understanding of the riches of their history. At times, the memoirs have become a jumping-off place for her fiction. She has a master's degree in English (in the "Emphasis on Writing Program") from the University of Minnesota. She lives in a suburb of Minneapolis, Minnesota, surrounded by "four terrific grandchildren who seem to enjoy hearing the family's stories."

WANDA J. PACE, TEMECULA, CALIFORNIA

Wanda MacDougall Pace was raised in Colorado and Southern California. She says she has loved reading all of her life, and has been a writer since she was young. She is a mother and grandmother, and treasures the history of past generations of her family.

MAUDE I. PARKER, BROOKLYN, NEW YORK

Maude I. Parker, R.N., B.S., M.A., was born in New York City to British West Indian parents. She is a lifelong resident and lover of that city. She has written poetry and short stories since childhood. She has been a teacher and supervisor of nursing, a pioneering supervisor of sex education, and an assistant director of work-experience training programs for high school students. Ms. Parker's writings have been published in nursing journals and sex-education journals. Her poetry appears in the anthology _Voices of Brooklyn_. Her poems have been published by the _St. Francis College Review_, the _University of Iowa Elderhostelers_, _Brooklyn Women_, and _Brooklyn College IRPE: Poetic Voices_. Ms. Parker is a member of the Afro-American Historical and Genealogical Society chapter in New York City. While history and genealogy are prime interests, she finds time for travel and photography as well. She is actively involved in the local YWCA and in her family-reunion association.

Marian Bailey Presswood, Benton, Tennessee

Ms. Presswood, a retired educator, is the official historian for Polk County, Tennessee; the reorganizer and president of the Polk County Historical & Genealogical Society; and the editor of the society's award-winning quarterly/newsletter. She established a genealogy library eight years ago, and serves as the four-day-a-week volunteer and head librarian. Ms. Presswood became interested in genealogy in the early 1990s at the request of her then-ninety-year-old father, who knew very little about his family history. Like most genealogists, she became "hooked," and now does family histories for a multitude of people all across the U.S., who contact her via e-mail, letters, and visits to the library. Her articles have received two awards in the Southern California Genealogical Society's Writing Contest.

William Lewis Principe, Jr., La Cañada-Flintridge, California

Mr. Principe is a board-certified professional genealogist specializing in New England and California Gold Rush families, as well as families of Italian ancestry. He has published articles in many professional genealogy journals, including <u>The American Genealogist</u> and the <u>New Hampshire Genealogical Record</u>. He is a member of the Society of the Cincinnati in the State of Rhode Island, the Sons of the Revolution in the State of California, the Society of California Pioneers, and the General Society of Mayflower Descendants. He earned a BA degree from the University of California, Berkeley, and an MBA degree from UCLA. He lives in Southern California with his wife, Kathleen, who is also an enthusiastic genealogist. For recreation, Bill and Kathleen are avid birders.

Leslie Prpich, Victoria, British Columbia, Canada

Ms. Prpich is a freelance writer and editor who lives on Vancouver Island with her partner and two sons. She has been imagining the lives of her ancestors in Croatia, Sweden, and

Staffordshire, England, since 1982.

VICKI RENFROE, ALVIN, TEXAS

Ms. Renfroe lives thirty miles south of Houston, the mother of five children and grandmother of six. She tell us: "Being a grandmother is tremendously more fun!!" She writes as a hobby, and recently learned that a novel she wrote eight years ago will be published next year. It is called <u>Hearts of the Children</u>, and follows four generations of women in one family, a story "loosely based on [her] own family history." The goal of the book is "to show how we pass down a lot more than our DNA to our children." She has taught math, science, and journalism for five years in a private school, and is now attending college at night to obtain her teaching certificate. She hopes to teach high school math starting this fall. She is currently employed as an engineering tech at a lithium-battery research and development plant. She has been a genealogist since 1976.

JOHN SHEIRER, ENFIELD, CONNECTICUT

John Sheirer teaches public speaking, writing, and literature at Asnuntuck Community College in Enfield, Connecticut, where he has been named to <u>Who's Who Among America's Teachers</u>. A Pushcart Prize nominee and finalist for the Sante Fe Writers Project Literary Awards, his writing has been published in <u>Clean Sheets</u>, <u>Clever</u>, <u>The Christian Science Monitor</u>, <u>Ethical Oasis</u>, <u>Faculty Shack</u>, <u>The Foliate Oak</u>, <u>Freshwater</u>, <u>Full Circle</u>, <u>Laughter Loaf</u>, <u>Modern Haiku</u>, <u>Nights and Weekends</u>, <u>Pinedeldyboz</u>, <u>Raw Nervz</u>, <u>Seven Seas Magazine</u>, <u>Still</u>, <u>Teaching English at the Two-Year College</u>, and <u>Word Riot</u>, among others. His books include <u>Shut Up and Speak!</u> (textbook), <u>Saying My Name</u> (poems), and <u>Free Chairs</u> (essays and stories). His newest book is a memoir, <u>Growing Up Mostly Normal in the Middle of Nowhere</u>. He is also an avid photographer who does volunteer work for land preservation with the Northern Connecticut Land Trust.

SHELLEY SIMON, SEATTLE, WASHINGTON

Mr. Simon writes: "I have worked as a singer/guitarist, restaurant owner, cowhand, handyman, systems analyst, computer programmer, claims adjuster, accountant, auditor, mailman, deli counterman, fountain boy, newspaper boy, and lemonade stand operator—more of a career romp than a career path. Currently I'm retired, but occasionally work as a street musician. And while trying my hand at writing, have had several articles published in Seattle's *Queen Anne News*. I completed my memoir nine months ago and it will certainly be published as soon as my name is legally changed to Bob Dylan."

GEORGE SMITH, DUNBARTONSHIRE, SCOTLAND

Mr. Smith was born in Glasgow, raised there, and has lived in the area all his life. He spent fifteen years as an engineer officer in the Merchant Navy in North America, Africa, the Indian sub-contineinent, the Persian Gulf, and Europe. When he came ashore, he worked in the maintenance department of the Polaroid factory for twenty-five years. He has been married to the same "long-suffering wife" for thirty-five years. His wife is from Newfoundland, and he has a son in Australia, and a married daughter in Paisley. He took up genealogy when he retired "to pass the time in the winter." He enjoys hillwalking. "We live right on the edge of the greater Glasgow area conurbastion, ten miles from Loch Lomond," he writes.

JEAN CHAPMAN SNOW, SHERMAN OAKS, CALIFORNIA

Ms. Snow is a teacher, freelance writer, and lecturer with editorial experience in newsletters and quarterlies. She earned her BA and MA in French and English from New York State College for Teachers (now SUNY, Albany), and has additional credits from New York and Southampton universities, Adelphi-Suffolk Community College (NY), Amherst College (MA), and Tacoma Community College (WA). She translated *A History of Medieval Latin Literature* by Engby Maurice Helin (New

York. *William Salloch, 1948), from French to English, was a columnist for the <u>Chapman Family Association Quarterly</u>, and is a columnist for <u>The Searcher</u> and the facilitator for the SCGS Writer's Group. Her articles have appeared in <u>Heritage Quest</u>, <u>American Astrology</u>, <u>Doll World</u>, <u>The Christian Science Monitor</u>, the <u>Los Angeles Times</u> and other newspapers, and a variety of other magazines. She has also won several prizes for poetry. After winning prizes for four years running in the SCGS Family History Writing Contest, she served as one of the contest judges in 2004.*

KATHLEEN (KAY) STEIN, LOS ANGELES, CALIFORNIA

Ms. Stein was born in London during the first World War, and lived there throughout World War II, during the "Blitz." She came to America in 1959 with her four children. She now has thirty-one descendants, including great-great-grandchildren. She says: "I've been writing my memoirs as bedtime stories for my grandchildren. <u>A Special Place</u> is one of them. My great-gran (or 'Nan' as we called her) lived to be ninety-eight, and was working in the field a week before she died of pleurisy. She was Maria Bicknell in the story, my paternal great-granma. My maternal granma died at age thirty-three, and that's why I got into genealogy. I wanted to find her parents, and I have been very lucky so far, in finding some of the descendants in Staffordshire, England. When I entered the genealogy competition, it was the first time. I felt honored to have the award and I do thank you."

WILSON ROBERT THORNLEY, (DECEASED)

Mr. Thornley's niece, Janis Lapides, writes of her late uncle: "[He] was a renowned creative writing teacher and published author. In his article, <u>The Case for Creative Writing</u>, he helped to start a revolution in the attitudes of teachers, administrators, and the public toward the evolving of special creative writing classes in high schools. In 1955, Mr. Thornley taught the only

special creative writing class in the state of Utah. . . . Mr.
Thornley's classes won more awards in the National Scholastic
Writing Awards contests than any other classes in the country.
His classes . . . were exciting partly because of the creative
process he revealed, and partly because of the warmth of his
humor. . . . His jokes, unprepared and unexpected, became part
of the lesson. In the process of learning to write, his students
learned how to live."

JACK VOGELSANG, OCEANSIDE, CALIFORNIA

Mr. Vogelsang was born in 1930 in Batavia (now Jakarta),
the capital of the former Dutch East Indies (Indonesia). After
being separated from his parents in a concentration camp for
two years and released ill from starvation, chronic malaria, and
tuberculosis, (his release is described in the article, <u>My Journey</u>
<u>to Freedom</u>), he was cared for by the Red Cross until he was
reunited with his parents six months after gaining his freedom.
He resumed his education in the fifth grade at the age of
seventeen. His family was repatriated to the Netherlands in
1950, where he spent a year and a half in a sanatarium
recovering from his illnesses. In 1956, he graduated with a bach-
elor's degree in mechanical engineering from an Amsterdam uni-
versity. He married, and the couple moved to the U.S. in 1959,
and in 1964 became U.S. citizens. His two children were both
born in the U.S. As a project manager for Rockwell, he worked
in Iran until that country's revolution, then worked in Saudi
Arabia until 1983. He was a a chief engineer with the U.N's
Interim Peace Keeping Forces in Lebanon until the mandatory
retirement ago of sixty, but was re-activated shortly thereafter,
and assigned to Morocco until 1993. Now permanently retired,
he lives with his wife near San Diego, and spends his time in
watercolor painting, writing, fishing, and travel.

KATHERINE YAMADA, GLENDALE, CALIFORNIA

Ms. Yamada writes a column for the <u>Glendale News-Press</u>, "Verdugo Views," focusing on people who have been important in Glendale's history. She is currently editing a new edition of the <u>Glendale Pictorial History Book</u> in preparation for Glendale's one-hundredth birthday on February 6, 2006. She has "searched for her roots" in Holland, Prussia, and Russia, and later took a similar trip to Japan in search of her husband's roots. Since then, she has finished three family-history books and is beginning a fourth. She and her husband, Glenn, enjoy nature travel, and have birded or fished on six continents. They have two daughters and three grandchildren.

STEPHEN A. YUNG, DOWNEY, CALIFORNIA

Mr. Yung was born in Oxnard, California, to California-born parents. He worked for thirty-five years with Security Pacific National Bank, which eventually became part of the Bank of America. He graduated from the University of Redlands in 1961, and has an MBA from the Wharton School. He retired early, in 1989, and, not being a golfer or fisherman, he looked for an avocation. His cousin had done a great deal of genealogy on the Coultas side of the family, so he thought genealogy might keep him occupied for a while. It has turned into a wonderful occupation, he writes. He has visited the birthplace of the Jungs in France, the Coultasses and Chamberlains in England, and to his wife, Lois', roots in Italy. He and his wife have been married for forty years and have two married children (both of whom are college teachers) and two grandsons.

About the Editor

BETH MALTBIE UYEHARA, RESEDA, CALIFORNIA

Before her retirement in 2001, Ms. Uyehara was, variously, a section editor, copy editor, and feature writer for the Los Angeles Times Special Sections department and the Los Angeles Times Syndicate. Previously, she had been the news editor of the Glendale News-Press, and the city editor of the Foothill Leader. She began genealogical research in 1994 to answer one simple question: Who was older, her grandmother or her great-aunt Lizzie? Every genealogist knows what happened next: By the time she answered that question, she had two dozen more—and she is still whacking away at the genealogical Hydra eleven years later. Ms. Uyehara wrote an occasional column, The Worm's Eye View of Genealogy, for the pioneering genealogy e-zine Missing Links, edited by Myra Vanderpool Gormley and Julie Case; the columns were published as The Zen of Genealogy (Heritage Books, 2002). She was featured in the Ancestors show on PBS, and for five years edited the SCGS quarterly, The Searcher. She also founded the SCGS Writer's Group and the SCGS Family History Writing Contest, on which this anthology is based. She shares a studio with her artist husband, Paul, and their three overfed, under-grateful cats.

Permissions

We thank the following publications for permission to reprint the below-mentioned articles in this anthology.

The Glendale News-Press, Glendale, California, originally published *Search for Roots* (Page 47). It is reprinted here with their permission.

The State Journal-Register, Springfield, Illinois, originally published *Coffee, Donuts, and Stamina: Clubmobiling in World War II* (Page 194). It is reprinted here with their permission.

Phoebe: Gender & Cultural Critiques, Vol 10/No. 1 (Spring 1998) published *Going to the Dance* (Page 10). It is reprinted here with their permission.

Senior Magazine originally published *A Shepherd Hears the Angels' Song* (Page 141) in December, 1999. *Senior Magazine* is no longer publishing, and the story is included here with the permission of the author.

In addition, the following stories were originally published in the So. Calif. Genealogical Society journal, *The Searcher,* and are reprinted with permission: *Touching Yesterday* (Page 50); *Tracing My African-American Ancestors* (Page 70); *Imagining Sam Burgess* (Page 81); *My 111 Years in a Danish Village* (Page 87); *A Minor Battle of the Revolutionary War* (Page 93); *Seeking Truth & Balance* (Page 99); *Aunt Mabel's Outhouse* (Page 113); *Names of Yore* (Page 121); *Margaret's Triumph* (Page 161); and *Family Gifts* (Page 175).

All page numbers refer to this anthology.

Name Index

237

GORMLEY, Myra
Vanderpool: 250
GOWER, Ann: 56
GRANT, _____: 157
GRANT, Peter: 158, 160
GRIFFITH, Jane: 58
GRIFFITH, John M.: 152, 153,
155
GRIFFITH, Zilpha Jane: 152
GROSSBERGER, Chajim Jozsef:
26
HALE, Dorsetta: *vi*, 208, 239
HALEY, Alex: 99
HAMMARSKJOLD, Dag: 212
HANSON, Willis T. Jr.: 98
HANSON, Norma Ann: *v*, 113,
239
HARMON, Dib: 28, 29, 30, 32
HARRIS, John, Colonel: 165
HARRIS, Kenneth F.: *v*, 125,
239
HARRIS, Phyllis I.T.: *vi*, 212,
239
HARRISON, J. F. C.: 81, 86
HAYS, Samuel: 165
HELIN, Maurice: 246
HERING, Bob: 206
HERRON, James E.: 165
HICKOX, Clarice: 194, 195,
196, 197, 198, 199, 200
HICKOX, H.L.: 196
HICKOX, H.V.: 196
HILL, Lauren: 211
HITLER, Adolf: 170, 171, 180
HOGAN, William Jesse: 148,

149
HOLBIN, Adam: 186
HUGHES, Anne: 57
HUGHES, Edward: 57
HUGHES, Hugh: 57
HUMPHREYS, M.: 57
IRWIN, Kay: *vii*
IVANOFF, Agapia: 3
IVANOFF, Grandma: 2, 3, 5
JACOB (Prout slave): 103
JACKSON, Samuel L.: 211
JACKSON FIVE: 210
JAMES (Prout slave): 103
JOHN, King: 34
JOHNSON, Sir John: 95
JONES, D. Elwern: *iv*, 55, 240
JONES, Charity (Chamberlain):
66, 67, 68
JONES, Thomas: 57
KAY, Ann: 122
KAY, Carl B.: 124
KAY, Charles Abner: 122
KAY, Emma: 122
KAY, Ernest: 122
KAY, Henrietta: 122
KAY, James: 122
KAY, James E.: 124
KAY, Jeremiah A.: 124
KAY, Joel: 122
KAY, Luther: 122
KAY, Mamie: 122
KAY, Mary: 122
KAY, Nannie: 122
KAY, Robert: 122, 124
KAY, Silas: 122